$ .91

Divided Light:
Father and Son Poems

Divided Light:

Father and Son
Poems

**A Twentieth-Century
American Anthology**

Edited by Jason Shinder

**The Sheep Meadow Press
Riverdale-on-Hudson, New York**

© 1983 by The Sheep Meadow Press. All rights reserved. Published 1983

Printed in the United States of America

The Sheep Meadow Press, Riverdale-on-Hudson, NY
Distributed by New Amsterdam Books
171 Madison Avenue, New York, NY 10016

Library of Congress Cataloging in Publication Data
Main entry under title:

Divided light.

  Bibliography: p.
    1. American poetry–20th century. 2. Fathers and sons–Poetry.
3. American poetry–Men authors.
I. Shinder, Jason, 1955–
PS595.F39D58 1983   811′.5′080354   83-18449
ISBN 0-935296-47-6 (pbk.)

Editor's Note

This is the first anthology to present poetry exclusively by American fathers and sons on the father and son relationship. The collection includes only those American father-son poems written during the twentieth century.

The poets are arranged chronologically. Where a poet is represented by more than one poem, the poems are arranged in order of their publication. Thus, the reader may follow the lines of development in the father-son poetry of individual poets, as well as trace the development of the father-son genre in twentieth-century American poetry.

My thanks go to the many poets whose work appears in this collection; for their support, patience, and generosity. Many of the contributors or their families, estates, or publishers offered father and son poems and photographs that were unknown or unavailable to me. Particular thanks for these reasons go to Karl Shapiro, Allen Ginsberg, Galway Kinnell, Carolyn Forché, Star Black, Jeff Lipkis, Martha Friedburg, and especially Stanley Kunitz and The Fine Arts Work Center in Provincetown. My thanks also to Juanita Lieberman and Ronda Kasl for helping with matters of research, correspondence, permissions, and proofreading. To Steven Bauer and Samuel Kashner, my thanks for their always being there with their friendly encouragement, suggestions, and intelligence concerning all matters of the book. My thanks also to the book's publisher, Stanley Moss. His concern and exacting reading of the entire text was indispensable.

I also want to thank my mother, Edith, my grandmother, Fanny, my brother, Martin, and my sister, Nina, for their support, and for their special understanding of this particular book.

Jason Shinder

What thou lovest well remains,
                              the rest is dross
What thou lov'st well shall not be reft from thee
What thou lov'st well is thy true heritage

Ezra Pound

Contents

Introduction

On the 11th of February, in 1977, when I had been living in California almost a year, my father died. It felt as though my father's sudden death was only a prelude to something worse; perhaps an even more intense confinement and solitude than I often experienced. Life seemed to be saying, well, this is it, here is irreversible sorrow that will forever change the vision and direction of your life. In the past, I had been inclined to be angry and dissatisfied with my father for the conditions of his life, for the conditions of our lives. When his life had ended I began to wonder about that life and also, in a new way, to be apprehensive about my own.

I had known my father well. We got on decently, lovingly; partly because we shared in our different fashions the vices of hard work and stubborn ambition. Yet when he was dead I realized I had hardly really spoken to him. When he had been dead for a time I began to wish more and more that I had. It seemed typical of life in America, where opportunities, real and fancied, are thicker than anywhere else on the globe, that fathers and sons often have no time to talk to each other.

I remembered one of the few times in all our life together when we really spoke to each other.

It was a Friday night in spring. We were attending a memorial service at a nearby temple for a friend of the family, Rabbi Stein. I was in my second year of college, had been doing some writing and, on this occasion, wrote a brief eulogy. I had known Rabbi Stein well. Between my tenth and thirteenth year we often walked together, just the two of us, in a lively air of conversation, to and from Temple. It was said in the town of Merrick, Long Island, quite truthfully, that the congregation of the temple insisted the Rabbi leave because he did not possess a master's degree in education. On this note, Rabbi Stein left with his family for Israel. The decision of the congregation turned out to be a deadly one, for within a short time after leaving America,

Rabbi Stein died of a heart attack in South Africa working as a fund raiser for an Israeli Yeshiva.

After I delivered the eulogy, insisting that part of the responsibility for Rabbi Stein's death rested in the hands of the congregation, my father leaned over to me and said abruptly, "That's what I would have said, if I could have written it."

I was astonished at his statement—because it was a real statement of approval and recognition of me as a writer and person whose products might indeed have substance and purpose in a society dominated by market exchange and increasing acquisitions. I answered, "I know."

That was all we said. It was enough. It pointed the way toward discovering the terms on which we might further understand each other.

However, he died soon thereafter, and so we shall never discover such terms. My feelings toward him and his toward me can never be explored—at least not in the way I hoped to explore them, sitting across from each other at the dinner table. Whatever was between us would have to be discovered in some other way. That way became clearer to me as the years went on—through my own writing and through the writing of others. I found revealed again and again, especially in poems, the love between my father and me, as well as the anger, short-sightedness and dishonesty we were inclined to repress. I felt linked with other sons and fathers in their efforts to speak to each other, and began searching for more poetry on the subject. The poems became my allies, and it became more and more necessary to hold them together in an anthology.

My father was of the second generation of Russians in America. His father and mother, along with thousands of other Europeans, came to America in the early 1900's, and his was the first of the succeeding generations who never saw the landscape that their parents or grandparents called home.

He was born in Brooklyn, New York, and was already working there by the age of seven after his father died suddenly of a heart attack. Whenever I think of Brooklyn, I must also helplessly think of my father as a young boy, dressed in his Saturday best, and running errands for the local business-people. My father rarely mentioned his father, Max, except to say how he felt angry and abandoned after his father's death but didn't remember very much about him. Yet there was a picture of my grandfather in one of the family's photo albums. Upon discovering it I asked my father why he had not hung it on the wall, but he didn't answer.

My father was, I think, handsome. My memories of him, on his way to dinner with my mother, are of a rather charming man, proud and grinning. On those occasions he looked to me like a leading man in the movies; and he was, I discovered later, an actor in several movies made in Hollywood during the 1940's. He possessed, in fact, a certain leading man's ability to establish immediate contact with other people. There was something in him, groping, tentative, sensitive and always humorous, that surfaced when he was facing people and trying to befriend them, as he often did.

I began to wonder what it felt like for my father to have many friends, three children, automobiles, a lovely home, a boat, but rarely time to enjoy them. He used to make jokes about his working so hard that never, of course, seemed very funny to me. They could not have seemed very funny to him, either, or else our all too feeble responses to them would never have ended in such odd moments of silence. He spent great energy and achieved, to his own satisfaction and surprise, no small amount of success, but the success was punctuated by acute feelings of doubt and disappointment. He could not always understand why, if he had so much energy to spare, he could not use it to make his life more and more enjoyable.

But the year that preceded my father's death did make important changes in his life, as well as in mine. I had been offered a teaching scholarship at the University of California at Davis, and he finally sold one of the restaurants he owned. He knew it was time to relax and begin changing the direction of his life. The best thing, he thought, was to take a vacation and have as little to do with his businesses as possible. Yet he didn't trust his decision and was always trying to find a reason not to leave. When it was clear my "education" was going to lead me to California, he then became interested in the possibility of living there.

Strangely, my father's plans began to suspend themselves, so to speak, in a certain helplessness and sadness. Later, after my father's death, I suspected in this sadness a meaning that had never been so clear to me before. It began to seem my father was struggling to hold two ideas in his mind that were in opposition to each other. The first idea was acceptance, acceptance of men as they are, of his life as it was and not as he expected or wished it to be. In light of this idea, it goes without saying that he would experience disappointments. But this did not mean he had to accept these disappointments as commonplace. For the second idea, of equal power and concern to him, was that he must try to understand and fight these disappointments with all of his energy. This struggle seemed to be laid in my hands after my father's death, and I've often wished he were beside me so that I could search his face for some of its understanding and strength.

I have worked on this anthology at such length not because it is my only subject, but because, like many of the book's contributors, the subject is the gate I had to unlock before I could hope to write and work fully on anything else.

For in my mind's eye I can always see my father sitting at the window of a phone booth in sunny Miami on the day of his death, locked up in his fears about finally taking a vacation when he had businesses to run, reaching toward one of his sons, who had left him by reaching toward the other side of the country. I often wonder what I would have said if I had been home and learned of his and my mother's wish to visit me.

I probably would not have said much, I think, in the oddest, most awful way. Later, confusing fantasy with reality, I thought I had somehow betrayed him, caused him his suffering and death. I lived it over and over again, the way one relives an automobile accident after it has happened, and one finds oneself alone but safe. I could not get over the fact that I would have said how busy I was with teaching, and that his visit would be wonderful but it would have to be brief. I see very clearly that I would have said this in order to fulfill what I thought was his idea of a strong, successful and loving son, and to keep the distance between us I was comfortable with.

The following morning I learned of my father's death. It lives in my mind as though it were the morning I contracted some dread, chronic illness—which was in part the learning of my own death. It was a kind of blind fever, a pounding in the skull and fire in the bowels. Once I contracted this fever I was never really cured of it, for the fever, without an instant's warning, recurs at any moment. It can surface while I am brushing my hair or in the middle of a conversation with a friend.

Somehow with the repetition of these scenes, which continue to ring in my head years after his death, I realized we would never meet again. He was no longer on the other side of the dinner table; there were, however, poems in which he kept surfacing. And when the poems were held together, the perpetual sorrow, confusion, and challenges posed by his life and sudden death, and by the experiences of other fathers and sons, were somehow, almost, perpetually met.

Jason Shinder
1983

Divided Light:
Father and Son Poems

Wallace Stevens

The Irish Cliffs of Moher

Who is my father in this world, in this house,
At the spirit's base?

My father's father, his father's father, his—
Shadows like winds

Go back to a parent before thought, before speech,
At the head of the past.

They go to the cliffs of Moher rising out of the mist,
Above the real,

Rising out of present time and place, above
The wet, green grass.

This is not landscape, full of the somnambulations
Of poetry

And the sea. This is my father or, maybe,
It is as he was,

A likeness, one of the race of fathers: earth
And sea and air.

William Carlos Williams

The Sparrow
(To My Father)

This sparrow
     who comes to sit at my window
        is a poetic truth
more than a natural one.
     His voice,
        his movements,

his habits—
        how he loves to
                flutter his wings
in the dust—
        all attest it;
                granted, he does it
to rid himself of lice
        but the relief he feels
                makes him
cry out lustily—
        which is a trait
                more related to music
than otherwise.
        Wherever he finds himself
                in early spring,
on back streets
        or beside palaces,
                he carries on
unaffectedly
        his amours.
                It begins in the egg,
his sex genders it:
        What is more pretentiously
                useless
or about which
        we more pride ourselves?
                It leads as often as not
to our undoing.
        The cockerel, the crow
                with their challenging voices
cannot surpass
        the insistence
                of his cheep!

Once
        at El Paso
                toward evening,
I saw—and heard!—
        ten thousand sparrows
                who had come in from
the desert
        to roost. They filled the trees
                of a small park. Men fled
(with ears ringing!)
        from their droppings,
                leaving the premises
to the alligators
        who inhabit
                the fountain. His image
is familiar
        as that of the aristocratic
                unicorn, a pity
there are not more oats eaten
        nowadays
                to make living easier
for him.
        At that,
                his small size,
keen eyes,
        serviceable beak
                and general truculence
assure his survival—
        to say nothing
                of his innumerable
brood.
        Even the Japanese
                know him
and have painted him
        sympathetically,
                with profound insight

into his minor
    characteristics.
        Nothing even remotely
subtle
    about his lovemaking.
        He crouches
before the female,
    drags his wings,
        waltzing,
throws back his head
    and simply—
        yells! The din
is terrific.
    The way he swipes his bill
        across a plank
to clean it,
    is decisive.
        So with everything
he does. His coppery
    eyebrows
        give him the air
of being always
    a winner—and yet
        I saw once,
the female of his species
    clinging determinedly
        to the edge of
a water pipe,
    catch him
        by his crown-feathers
to hold him
    silent,
        subdued,

hanging above the city streets
    until
        she was through with him.
What was the use
    of that?
        She hung there
herself,
    puzzled at her success.
        I laughed heartily.
Practical to the end,
    it is the poem
        of his existence
that triumphed
    finally;
        a wisp of feathers
flattened to the pavement,
    wings spread symmetrically
        as if in flight,
the head gone,
    the black escutcheon of the breast
        undecipherable,
an effigy of a sparrow,
    a dried wafer only,
        left to say
and it says it
    without offense,
        beautifully;
This was I,
    a sparrow.
        I did my best;
farewell.

William Carlos Williams

Address:

To a look in my son's eyes—
        I hope he did not see
                that I was looking—
that I have seen
        often enough
                in the mirror,
a male look
        approaching despair—
                there is a female look
to match it
        no need to speak of that:
                Perhaps
it was only a dreamy look
        not an unhappy one
                but absent
from the world—
        such as plagued the eyes
                of Bobby Burns
in his youth and threw him
        into the arms
                of women—
in which he could
        forget himself,
                not defiantly,
but with full acceptance
        of his lot
                as a man
His Jean forgave him
        and took him to her heart
                time after time
when he would be
        too drunk
                with Scotch

or the love of other women
        to notice
                what he was doing.
What was he intent upon
        but to drown out
                that look? What
does it portend?
        A war
                will not erase it
nor a bank account,
        estlin,
                amounting to 9 figures.
Flow gently sweet Afton
        among thy green braes—
                no matter
that he wrote the song
        to another woman
                it was never for sale.

E.E. Cummings

my father moved through dooms of love

my father moved through dooms of love
through sames of am through haves of give,
singing each morning out of each night
my father moved through depths of height

this motionless forgetful where
turned at his glance to shining here;
that if (so timid air is firm)
under his eyes would stir and squirm

newly as from unburied which
floats the first who, his april touch
drove sleeping selves to swarm their fates
woke dreamers to their ghostly roots

and should some why completely weep
my father's fingers brought her sleep:
vainly no smallest voice might cry
for he could feel the mountains grow.

Lifting the valleys of the sea
my father moved through griefs of joy;
praising a forehead called the moon
singing desire into begin

joy was his song and joy so pure
a heart of star by him could steer
and pure so now and now so yes
the wrists of twilight would rejoice

keen as midsummer's keen beyond
conceiving mind of sun will stand,
so strictly (over utmost him
so hugely) stood my father's dream

his flesh was flesh his blood was blood:
no hungry man but wished him food;
no cripple wouldn't creep one mile
uphill to only see him smile.

Scorning the pomp of must and shall
my father moved through dooms of feel;
his anger was as right as rain
his pity was as green as grain

septembering arms of year extend
less humbly wealth to foe and friend

than he to foolish and to wise
offered immeasurable is

proudly and (by octobering flame
beckoned) as earth will downward climb,
so naked for immortal work
his shoulders marched against the dark

his sorrow was as true as bread:
no liar looked him in the head;
if every friend became his foe
he'd laugh and build a world with snow.

My father moved through theys of we,
singing each new leaf out of each tree
(and every child was sure that spring
danced when she heard my father sing)

then let men kill which cannot share,
let blood and flesh be mud and mire,
scheming imagine, passion willed,
freedom a drug that's bought and sold

giving to steal and cruel kind,
a heart to fear, to doubt a mind,
to differ a disease of same,
conform the pinnacle of am

though dull were all we taste as bright,
bitter all utterly things sweet,
maggoty minus and dumb death
all we inherit, all bequeath

and nothing quite so least as truth
—i say though hate were why men breathe—
because my father lived his soul
love is the whole and more than all

John Hall Wheelock

The Gardener

Father, whom I knew well for forty years,
Yet never knew, I have come to know you now—
In age, make good at last those old arrears.

Though time that snows the hair and lines the brow
Has equalled us, it was not time alone
That brought me to the knowledge I here avow.

Some profound divination of your own
In all the natural effects you sought
Planted a secret that is now made known.

These woodland ways, with your heart's labor bought,
Trees that you nurtured, gardens that you planned,
Surround me here, mute symbols of your thought.

Your meaning beckons me on every hand;
Grave aisles and vistas, in their silence, speak
A language which I now can understand.

In all you did, as in yourself, unique—
Servant of beauty, whom I seek to know,
Discovering here the clue to what I seek.

When down the nave of your great elms I go
That soar their Gothic arches where the sky,
Nevertheless, with all its stars will show,

Or when the moon of summer, riding high,
Spills through the leaves her light from far away,
I feel we share the secret, you and I.

All these you loved and left. We may not stay
Long with the joy our hearts are set upon:
This is a thing that here you tried to say.

The night has fallen; the day's work is done;
Your groves, your lawns, the passion of this place
Cry out your love of them—but you are gone.

O father, whom I may no more embrace
In childish fervor, but, standing far apart,
Look on your spirit rather than your face,

Time now has touched me also, and my heart
Has learned a sadness that yours earlier knew,
Who labored here, though with the greater art.

The truth is on me now that was with you:
How life is sweet, even its very pain,
The years how fleeting and the days how few.

Truly, your labors have not been in vain;
These woods, these walks, these gardens—everywhere
I look, the glories of your love remain.

Therefore, for you, now beyond praise or prayer,
Before the night falls that shall make us one,
In which neither of us will know or care,

This kiss, father, from him who was your son.

Robinson Jeffers

To His Father

Christ was your lord and captain all your life,
He fails the world but you he did not fail,
He led you through all forms of grief and strife
Intact, a man full-armed, he let prevail

Nor outward malice nor the worse-fanged snake
That coils in one's own brain against your calm,
That great rich jewel well guarded for his sake
With coronal age and death like quieting balm.
I Father having followed other guides
And oftener to my hurt no leader at all,
Through years nailed up like dripping panther hides
For trophies on a savage temple wall
Hardly anticipate that reverend stage
Of life, the snow-wreathed honor of extreme age.

Charles Reznikoff

Five Groups of Verse

32

He was afraid to go through their grocery store, where his
   father was still talking to customers. He went through the
   tenement hallway into the room where they ate and slept,
   in back of the store.
His little brothers and sisters were asleep along the big bed.
   He took the book which he had bought at a pushcart, to
   read just a page or two more by the dimmed gaslight.
His father stood over him and punched his head twice,
whispering in Yiddish, "Where have you been lost all day,
   you louse that feeds on me? I needed you to deliver
   orders."
In the dawn he carried milk and rolls to the doors of
   customers. At seven he was in his chum's room. "I'll stay
   here with you till I get a job."

He worked for a printer. When he was twenty-one he set up a press in a basement. It was harder to pay off than he had thought.

He fell behind in his installments. If they took the press away, he would have to work for someone else all over again.

Rosh Ha-Shonoh he went to his father's house. They had been speaking to each other again for years.

Once a friend had turned a poem of his into Hebrew. It was printed in a Hebrew magazine. He showed it to his father, and his father showed it around to the neighbors.

After dinner his father said, "Business has been good, thank God. I have saved over a thousand dollars this year. How have you been doing?"

"Well." "But I hear that you need money, that you're trying to borrow some?" "Yes." His father paused. "I hope you get it."

35

A Son with a Future

When he was four years old, he stood at the window during a thunderstorm. His father, a tailor, sat on the table sewing. He came up to his father and said, "I know what makes thunder: two clouds knock together."

When he was older, he recited well-known rants at parties. They all said that he would be a lawyer.

At law school he won a prize for an essay. Afterwards, he became the chum of an only son of rich people. They were said to think the world of the young lawyer.

The Appellate Division considered the matter of his disbarment. His relatives heard rumours of embezzlement.

When a boy, to keep himself at school, he had worked in a drug store.

Now he turned to this half-forgotten work, among perfumes and pungent drugs, quiet after the hubble-bubble of the courts and the search in law books.

He had just enough money to buy a drug store in a side
    street.

Influenza broke out. The old tailor was still keeping his shop
    and sitting cross-legged on the table sewing, but he was
    half-blind.
He, too, was taken sick. As he lay in bed he thought, "What a
    lot of money doctors and druggists must be making; now
    is my son's chance."
They did not tell him that his son was dead of influenza.

John Wheelwright

Father

An East Wind asperges Boston with Lynn's sulphurous
    brine.
Under the bridge of turrets my father built,—from turning
    sign
of CHEVROLET, out-topping our gilt State House dome
to burning sign of CARTER'S INK,—drip multitudes
of checker-board shadows. Inverted turreted reflections
sleeting over axle-grease billows, through all directions
cross-cut parliamentary gulls, who toss like gourds.

> Speak. Speak to me again, as fresh saddle leather
> (Speak; talk again) to a hunter smells of heather.
> Come home. Wire a wire of warning without words.
> Come home and talk to me again, my first friend.
>   Father,
> come home, dead man, who made your mind my home.

Richard Eberhart

Father and Son

| Father | Could you catch a little fish, Son, |
| | Could you catch a little fish? |

Son	Yes, Father, I could catch a little fish,
	A little fish, Father, catch,
	But I must do it in my own way.

| Father | But I have got the proper hook, Son, |
| | I have got the proper book of hooks. |

Son	Let me cast it my own way, Father,
	I will not get the line caught in the reel.
	Let me catch, Father, fetch the fish.

| Father | Son, catch the fish the way I say, Son, |
| | Hold the line up fair and fine from the river. |

Son	I have a bobbin, Father, I have a bobbin,
	See my bobbin swirling in the rapids, Father,
	I like to let my line down for the fish to see.

| Father | Quickly, Son, pull the line in quick, Son. |
| | Don't be a laggard when the fish may pull. |

Son	I will await my time, my time await, Father,
	I have never put my hook herein before,
	Let me, Father, let me dawdle by the shore.

| Father | You've fouled the reel, Son, the reel already. |
| | Take out the bait and straighten, I'll help you straighten. |

Son	But, Father, I have got to catch a little fish,
	I feel a fish is waiting under for my line.
	Let me do it my way, Father, my way.

| Father | Leave the hook and bobbin in the swirling river |
| | And may you catch a little fish, a little fish today. |

Son	They say they bite when there is nearly thunder.
	My crisp creel is waiting for the advent, Father,
	I want to net a vivid fish today.
Father	No doubt we have come here too late in the day.
	Son, come home, give up the quest, and come away.
Son	Such pleasure it is to dawdle by the river,
	I'll come if, come away if, come if, Father,
	If only a fish will bite upon my line.
Father	I said to pull your line in, pull, and come away.
	Pull in the bobbin, flat, and wind in the reel.
Son	If this is a command, Father, I'll come away.
	But fish must be in the river, fish for me.
	And if there are none for you, I'm sorry, Father, sorry.
Father	Then come, I'll take you home, you home, take,
	I'll take you safely from the rapids and the river.
Son	I'll catch the fish that you have never caught, Father.
	I'll catch the fish, bobbing fish, in my own way.
	If you will only wait and watch, and wait and see.
Father	Some say the fish are endless in the sea.
	There is a spawn of life beyond our wills.
Son	My fish are what I wish to catch, Father, own fish,
	Now help me up the bank, me help, now help,
	Father. You brought me, now you take me back.

Stanley Kunitz

For the Word is Flesh

O ruined father dead, long sweetly rotten
Under the dial, the time-dissolving urn,
Beware a second perishing, forgotten,
Heap fallen leaves of memory to burn
On the slippery rock, the black eroding heart,
Before the wedged frost splits it clean apart.

The nude hand drops no sacramental flower
Of blood among the tough upthrusting weeds.
Senior, in this commemorative hour,
What shall the quick commemorate, what deeds
Ephemeral, what dazzling words that flare
Like rockets from the mouth to burst in air?

Of hypochondriacs that gnawed their seasons
In search of proofs, Lessius found twenty-two
Fine arguments, Tolet gave sixty reasons
Why souls survive. And what are they to you?
And, father, what to me, who cannot blur
The mirrored brain with fantasies of Er,

Remembering such factual spikes as pierce
The supplicating palms, and by the sea
Remembering the eyes, I hear the fierce
Wild cry of Jesus on the holy tree,
Yet have of you no syllable to keep,
Only the deep rock crumbling in the deep.

Observe the wisdom of the Florentine
Who, feeling death upon him, scribbled fast
To make revision of a deathbed scene,
Gloating that he was accurate at last.
Let sons learn from their lipless fathers how
Man enters hell without a golden bough.

Stanley Kunitz

Father and Son

Now in the suburbs and the falling light
I followed him, and now down sandy road
Whiter than bone-dust, through the sweet
Curdle of fields, where the plums
Dropped with their load of ripeness, one by one.
Mile after mile I followed, with skimming feet,
After the secret master of my blood,
Him, steeped in the odor of ponds, whose indomitable love
Kept me in chains. Strode years; stretched into bird;
Raced through the sleeping country where I was young,
The silence unrolling before me as I came,
The night nailed like an orange to my brow.

How should I tell him my fable and the fears,
How bridge the chasm in a casual tone,
Saying, "The house, the stucco one you built,
We lost. Sister married and went from home,
And nothing comes back, it's strange, from where she goes.
I lived on a hill that had too many rooms:
Light we could make, but not enough of warmth,
And when the light failed, I climbed under the hill.
The papers are delivered every day;
I am alone and never shed a tear."

At the water's edge, where the smothering ferns lifted
Their arms, "Father!" I cried, "Return! You know
The way. I'll wipe the mudstains from your clothes;
No trace, I promise, will remain. Instruct
Your son, whirling between two wars,
In the Gemara of your gentleness,
For I would be a child to those who mourn
And brother to the foundlings of the field

And friend of innocence and all bright eyes.
O teach me how to work and keep me kind."

Among the turtles and the lilies he turned to me
The white ignorant hollow of his face.

Stanley Kunitz

The Portrait

My mother never forgave my father
for killing himself,
especially at such an awkward time
and in a public park,
that spring
when I was waiting to be born.
She locked his name
in her deepest cabinet
and would not let him out,
though I could hear him thumping.
When I came down from the attic
with the pastel portrait in my hand
of a long-lipped stranger
with a brave moustache
and deep brown level eyes,
she ripped it into shreds
without a single word
and slapped me hard.
In my sixty-fourth year
I can feel my cheek
still burning.

Stanley Kunitz

Quinnapoxet

I was fishing in the abandoned reservoir
back in Quinnapoxet,
where the snapping turtles cruised
and the bullheads swayed
in their bower of tree-stumps,
sleek as eels and pigeon-fat.
One of them gashed my thumb
with a flick of his razor fin
when I yanked the barb
out of his gullet.
The sun hung its terrible coals
over Buteau's farm: I saw
the treetops seething.

They came suddenly into view
on the Indian road,
evenly stepping
past the apple orchard,
commingling with the dust
they raised, their cloud of being,
against the dripping light
looming larger and bolder.
She was wearing a mourning bonnet
and a wrap of shining taffeta.
"Why don't you write?" she cried
from the folds of her veil.
"We never hear from you."
I had nothing to say to her.
But for him who walked behind her
in his dark worsted suit,
with his face averted
as if to hide a scald,

deep in his other life,
I touched my forehead
with my swollen thumb
and splayed my fingers out—
in deaf-mute country
the sign for father.

Robert Penn Warren

After Night Flight
  (Mortmain: I)

> *After Night Flight Son Reaches Bedside of Already Un-*
> *conscious Father, Whose Right Hand Lifts in a Spasmodic*
> *Gesture, as Though Trying to Make Contact: 1955*

In Time's concatenation and
Carnal conventicle, I,
Arriving, being flung through dark and
The abstract flight-grid of sky,
Saw rising from the sweated sheet and
Ruck of bedclothes ritualistically
Reordered by the paid hand
Of mercy—saw rising the hand—

Christ, start again! What was it I,
Standing there, travel-shaken, saw
Rising? What could it be that I,
Caught sudden in gut- or conscience-gnaw,
Saw rising out of the past, which I
Saw now as twisted bedclothes? Like law,
The hand rose cold from History
To claw at a star in the black sky,

But could not reach that far—oh, cannot!
And the star horribly burned, burns,
For in darkness the wax-white clutch could not
Reach it, and white hand on wrist-stem turns,
Lifts in last tension of tendon, but cannot
Make contact—*oh, oop-si-daisy,* churns
The sad heart, *oh, atta-boy, daddio's got
One more shot in the locker, peas-porridge hot—*

But no. Like an eyelid the hand sank, strove
Downward, and in that darkening roar,
All things—all joy and the hope that strove,
The failed exam, the admired endeavor,
Prizes and prinkings, and the truth that strove,
And back of the Capitol, boyhood's first whore—
Were snatched from me, and I could not move,
Naked in that black blast of his love.

Robert Penn Warren

Promises
To Gabriel

    I
*What Was the Promise that Smiled from
the Maples at Evening?*

What was the promise that smiled from the maples at
    evening?
Smiling dim from the shadow, recessed? What language of
    leaf-lip?

And the heels of the fathers click on the concrete, returning,
Each aware of his own unspecified burden, at sun-dip.
In first darkness hydrangeas float white in their spectral
    precinct.
Beneath pale hydrangeas the first firefly utters cold burning.
The sun is well down, the first star has now winked.

What was the promise when bullbats dizzied the sunset?
They skimmer and skitter in gold light at great height.
The guns of big boys on the common go *boom,* past regret.
Boys shout when the bullbat spins down in that gold light.
"Too little to shoot"—but next year you'll be a big boy.
So shout now and pick up the bird—why, that's blood, it is
    wet.
Its eyes are still open, your heart in the throat swells like joy.

What was the promise when, after the last light had died,
Children gravely, down walks, in spring dark, under maples,
    drew
Trains of shoe boxes, empty, with windows, with candles
    inside,
Going *chuck-chuck,* and blowing for crossings, lonely, *oo-oo?*
But on impulse you fled, and they called, called across the
    dark lawn,
Long calling your name, who now lay in the darkness to
    hide,
While the sad little trains glimmer on under maples, and on.

What was the promise when, after the dying was done,
All the long years before, like burnt paper, flared into black,
And the house shrunk to silence, the odor of flowers near
    gone?
Recollection of childhood was natural: cold gust at the back.
What door on the dark flings open, then suddenly bangs?
Yes, something was lost in between, but it's long, the way
    back.

25

You sleep, but in sleep hear a door that creaks where it
   hangs.

Long since, in a cold and coagulate evening, I've stood
Where they slept, the long dead, and the farms and far
   woods fled away,
And a gray light prevailed and both landscape and heart
   were subdued.
Then sudden, the ground at my feet was like glass, and I say
What I saw, saw deep down—with their fleshly habiliments
   rent,
But their bones in a phosphorus of glory agleam, there they
   lay,
Side by side, Ruth and Robert. But quickly that light was
   spent.

Earth was earth, and in earth-dark the glow died, therefore
   I lifted
My gaze to that world which had once been the heart's
   familiar,
Swell of woods and far field-sweep, in dusk by stream-
   gleams now wefted,
Railroad yonder and coal chute, town roofs far under the
   first star.
Then her voice, long forgotten, calm in silence, said:
   "Child."
And his, with the calm of a night field, or far star:
"We died only that every promise might be fulfilled."

George Oppen

Birthplace: New Rochelle

Returning to that house
And the rounded rocks of childhood—They have lasted
     well.

A world of things.

An aging man,
The knuckles of my hand
So jointed! I am this?

                    The house
My father's once, and the ground. There is a color of his
     times
In the sun's light.

A generation's mark.
It intervenes. My child,
Not now a child, our child
Not altogether lone in a lone universe that suffers time
Like stones in sun. For we do not.

Theodore Roethke

My Papa's Waltz

The whiskey on your breath
Could make a small boy dizzy;
But I hung on like death:
Such waltzing was not easy.

We romped until the pans
Slid from the kitchen shelf;

My mother's countenance
Could not unfrown itself.

The hand that held my wrist
Was battered on one knuckle;
At every step you missed
My right ear scraped a buckle.

You beat time on my head
With a palm caked hard by dirt,
Then waltzed me off to bed
Still clinging to your shirt.

Theodore Roethke

Otto

1

He was the youngest son of a strange brood,
A Prussian who learned early to be rude
To fools and frauds: He does not put on airs
Who lived above a potting shed for years.
I think of him, and I think of his men,
As close to him as any kith or kin.
Max Laurisch had the greenest thumb of all.
A florist does not woo the beautiful:
He potted plants as if he hated them.
What root of his ever denied its stem?
When flowers grew, their bloom extended him.

2

His hand could fit into a woman's glove,
And in a wood he knew whatever moved;
Once when he saw two poachers on his land,
He threw his rifle over with one hand;
Dry bark flew in their faces from his shot,—
He always knew what he was aiming at.
They stood there with their guns; he walked toward,
Without his rifle, and slapped each one hard;
It was no random act, for those two men
Had slaughtered game, and cut young fir trees down.
I was no more than seven at the time.

3

A house for flowers! House upon house they built,
Whether for love or out of obscure guilt
For ancestors who loved a warlike show,
Or Frenchmen killed a hundred years ago,
And yet still violent men, whose stacked-up guns
Killed every cat that neared their pheasant runs;
When Hattie Wright's angora died as well,
My father took it to her, by the tail.
Who loves the small can be both saint and boor,
(And some grow out of shape, their seed impure;)
The Indians loved him, and the Polish poor.

4

In my mind's eye I see those fields of glass,
As I looked out at them from the high house,
Riding beneath the moon, hid from the moon,
Then slowly breaking whiter in the dawn;
When George the watchman's lantern dropped from sight
The long pipes knocked: It was the end of night.
I'd stand upon my bed, a sleepless child
Watching the waking of my father's world.—
O world so far away! O my lost world!

Theodore Roethke

The Lost Son

1. The Flight

At Woodlawn I heard the dead cry:
I was lulled by the slamming of iron,
A slow drip over stones,
Toads brooding wells.
All the leaves stuck out their tongues;
I shook the softening chalk of my bones,
Saying,
Snail, snail, glister me forward,
Bird, soft-sigh me home,
Worm, be with me.
This is my hard time.

Fished in an old wound,
The soft pond of repose;
Nothing nibbled my line,
Not even the minnows came.

Sat in an empty house
Watching shadows crawl,
Scratching.
There was one fly.

Voice, come out of the silence.
Say something.
Appear in the form of a spider
Or a moth beating the curtain.

Tell me:
Which is the way I take;
Out of what door do I go,
Where and to whom?

Dark hollows said, lee to the wind,
The moon said, back of an eel,
The salt said, look by the sea,
Your tears are not enough praise,
You will find no comfort here,
In the kingdom of bang and blab.

Running lightly over spongy ground,
Past the pasture of flat stones,
The three elms,
The sheep strewn on a field,
Over a rickety bridge
Toward the quick-water, wrinkling and rippling.

Hunting along the river,
Down among the rubbish, the bug-riddled foliage,
By the muddy pond-edge, by the bog-holes,
By the shrunken lake, hunting, in the heat of summer.

The shape of a rat?
        It's bigger than that.
        It's less than a leg
        And more than a nose,
        Just under the water
        It usually goes.

2. *The Pit*

Where do the roots go?
    Look down under the leaves.
Who put the moss there?
    These stones have been here too long.
Who stunned the dirt into noise?
    Ask the mole, he knows.
I feel the slime of a wet nest.
    Beware Mother Mildew.
Nibble again, fish nerves.

3. *The Gibber*

At the wood's mouth,
By the cave's door,
I listened to something
I had heard before.

Dogs of the groin
Barked and howled,
The sun was against me,
The moon would not have me.

The weeds whined,
The snakes cried,
The cows and briars
Said to me: Die.

What a small song. What slow clouds. What dark water.
Hath the rain a father? All the caves are ice. Only the snow's
    here.
I'm cold. I'm cold all over. Rub me in father and mother.
Fear was my father, Father Fear.
His look drained the stones.

> What gliding shape
> Beckoning through halls,
> Stood poised on the stair,
> Fell dreamily down?
>
> From the mouths of jugs
> Perched on many shelves,
> I saw substance flowing
> That cold morning.
>
> Like a slither of eels
> That watery cheek

As my own tongue kissed
My lips awake.

Is this the storm's heart? The ground is unstilling itself.
My veins are running nowhere. Do the bones cast out their
        fire?
Is the seed leaving the old bed? These buds are live as birds.
Where, where are the tears of the world?
Let the kisses resound, flat like a butcher's palm;
Let the gestures freeze; our doom is already decided.
All the windows are burning! What's left of my life?
I want the old rage, the lash of primordial milk!
Goodbye, goodbye, old stones, the time-order is going,
I have married my hands to perpetual agitation,
I run, I run to the whistle of money.

Money money money
Water water water

How cool the grass is.
Has the bird left?
The stalk still sways.
Has the worm a shadow?
What do the clouds say?

These sweeps of light undo me.
Look, look, the ditch is running white!
I've more veins than a tree!
Kiss me, ashes, I'm falling through a dark swirl.

4. *The Return*

The way to the boiler was dark,
Dark all the way,
Over slippery cinders
Through the long greenhouse.

The roses kept breathing in the dark.
They had many mouths to breathe with.
My knees made little winds underneath
Where the weeds slept.

There was always a single light
Swinging by the fire-pit,
Where the fireman pulled out roses,
The big roses, the big bloody clinkers.

Once I stayed all night.
The light in the morning came slowly over the white
Snow.
There were many kinds of cool
Air.
Then came steam.

Pipe-knock.

Scurry of warm over small plants.
Ordnung! ordnung!
Papa is coming!

A fine haze moved off the leaves;
Frost melted on far panes;
The rose, the chrysanthemum turned toward the light.
Even the hushed forms, the bent yellowy weeds
Moved in a slow up-sway.

5. *"It was beginning winter"*

It was beginning winter,
An in-between time,
The landscape still partly brown:
The bones of weeds kept swinging in the wind,
Above the blue snow.

It was beginning winter,
The light moved slowly over the frozen field,
Over the dry seed-crowns,
The beautiful surviving bones
Swinging in the wind.

Light traveled over the wide field;
Stayed.
The weeds stopped swinging.
The mind moved, not alone,
Through the clear air, in the silence.

    Was it light?
    Was it light within?
    Was it light within light?
    Stillness becoming alive,
    Yet still?

A lively understandable spirit
Once entertained you.
It will come again.
Be still.
Wait.

James Agee

In Memory of My Father
(Campbell County, Tenn.)

allegretto

Bluely, bluely, styles from stone chimneys crippling smoke
of hickory larch and cedar wood of elm of the white oak.

The quell night blues above. The quell night blues:
Branchwaters, the black woods, begin to talk.

The blue night blacks above: Lamps:
Bloom in their glasses and the stars:
Splinter and glister glass. Warmth:
Slopes from the pigsty. In the barn pale hay,
Tusseled in teeth, darkness, a blunt hoof.

The black night blinds above. Tell me was ever love.
    so gentle in
the hand . so tender in the eye. was ever love. :
more lovely to the loved.

The secret water smiles upon herself; the blue cedar :
stands in his stone of smoke.
Mile on mile in mountain folded valley fallen   valley lies.
Eyes fixed on silence small owls preach forlorn   forlorn:
The metal thrill of frog and cricket thousands in the
    weltered grass:
Swinging his chain   the whippoorwill   the whippoorwill
    the answering chain:
Deepchested from his bowstring   a big frog bolts response :

              swinging his grieving chain

Cry, lonesome preacher : choir, shrill creatures of enamored de
amorous water, parsley, elapse : slow stars, display your edge
effortless air : love in the neat leaves   the neat leaves : gentl

Ben Belitt

Karamazov

1. Smerdyakov with a Guitar
"Who doesn't wish his father dead?"—Ivan Karamazov

I looked from the stair-well:
                          The scream
Of the feigned fall whirred in my throat,
No longer dissembled, and my mother arose from the dung,
Big with my outrage.
                          The cellar-door swung...

And I moved through an epilept's dream:
A guitar and a melon, floretted, a noose and a fang,
A cradle that pulsed like a heart and a crystal that sprang,
Showing my father, asleep in his spilth, in a streamer of gall,
His nakedness sparkling like alcohol...

And I lifted my birth, like a jawbone:
                                    "Is it now, Mother?"
I called to the stair-well: *"Mother, do we tumble him now?"*

—The melon-rind tightened, the strings of the fingerboard
      trembled—

And: *"Murderer!"* came in the pause: *"Would you murder the
      Husbandman? Bow!*
Bow!" said my mother: *"Bow down to the innocent cause!"*

So I beat on the rind with my jawbone
                                    and bowed to my father
And sang.

2. Alyosha's Funeral Service
"Instead of lenten oil, I will give you sucking pig and kasha."
—Karamazov

If the child's tooth
Fall on the unoffending finger, the finger
Bleeds for it, and the stone shows blood.

I am content with that.

                    It suffices for crucifixion.

It was corruption's smell that led me to my father,
A carrion way, through the saint's phosphorescence
And the faulting mind of my brother, to the incorruptible
    Presence,
Where, at the horn's end, awaiting the idiot Bringer,
A child's death babbles of dogs in an innocent fiction
And all things acknowledge the dissolute beast of the good.

Construe, little pigeons:
How we squandered that ruin of fathers,
And how the inexhaustible fathers restore us!
Old liars, dividing the verities,
Broken-haired mountebanks, eaters of cabbage and
    gudgeon,
Snoring in spittle and driving their murders before us,
Gods of the pestle and mortar and priests of the bludgeon,
Touching their thighs in an augury, and looking like
    youth—
Where was an end to their love?

                  When our violence faltered,
They contrived the empowering outrage to darken our
    knuckles
And accomplish their perfect destruction.

When we rose on the smoke of the sacrifice, vaunting our
    famine,
Fasted and absolute, crackling the crystals of salt,
They broke the abysses and showed us the bladders of
    salmon
Sowing the deluge like pollen.
                                    Their benevolence altered
The zenith's unsparing progressions and the span of the
    sickle,
Calling the figures of dread and credulity up
And shaping the seasons' similitudes for the lover:
The thread of the mayflower, beforehand, stilting a cup
On the scrolled leaf and the imminent foils of summer;
The skunk in the shorn grass, in chicory and clover
Forcing his whiteness under a ringing of stars;
The moth in a pathos of veins,
                                    cadaver of perishing color...

In whatever defiled or affronted us—
The coveter's rage that we dreamed on the beds of our
    neighbors,
Crimes, contradictions, enigmas, anomalies, wars,
Chance's inspired alternations at play with the possible,
Perfidies, nightmares, vendettas—they haunted us,
Demanding a parricide's justice to hallow their labors
And work the design of their voices.

Their gift was dismay and unreason: the saving enormity
That heeled on its instincts and bayed its intent, like a dog,
Grinding the gristle and bone of the spirit's deformity
And pursuing its will to perfection into the bog.

For their need was profane, like our own—
                                    a dream of abundance
In the lewd cornucopia's helix that bounds the abyss
And whirls the extremes of our will on its blinding
    redundance;

The rout of the priest and the scribe and the epilept beggar,
Beads, lacerations, and martyrdoms;
                              Armageddons, gardens;
The equivocal vision of judgment concealed in a parable
Where the intriguer's coffin waits, and the intriguer,
Forever uninnocent, sways toward the terrible wardens,
While over the leveling rifles,
A rider approaches upon the inquisitor's errand,
Bearing the pardon that murders, and the murder
     that pardons.

Paul Goodman

North Percy

11. Pagan Rites

Creator Spirit come
by whom
     I'll say what is real
     and so away I'll steal.

When my only son
fell down and died on Percy mountain
     I began
     to practice magic like a pagan.

Around the open grave we ate
the blueberries that he brought
     from the cloud, and then we
     buried his bag with his body.

Upon the covered grave
I laid the hawkweed that I love
    which withered fast
    where the mowers passed.

I brought also a tiny yellow
flower whose name I do not know
    to share my ignorance
    with my son. (But since

then I find in the book
it is a kind of shamrock
    Oxalis corniculata,
    Matty, sorrel of the lady.)

Blue-eyed grass with its gold hexagon
    beautiful as the gold and blue
    double in Albireo
that we used to gaze on

when Matty was alive
I laid on Matty's grave
    where two robins were
    hopping here and there;

and gold and bluer than that blue
or the double in Albireo
    bittersweet nightshade
    the deadly alkaloid
        I brought for no other reason
        than because it was poison.

Mostly, though, I brought some weed
beautiful but disesteemed,
    plantain or milkweed,
    because we die by the wayside.

(And if spring comes again
I will bring a dandelion,

because he was a common weed
and also he was splendid.)

But when I laid my own forehead
on the withering sod
to go the journey deep,
I could not fall asleep.

I cannot dream, I cannot quit
the one scene in the twilight
that is no longer new yet does
not pass into what was.

Last night the Pastoral Symphony
of Handel in the key of C
I played on our piano
out of tune shrill and slow

because the shepherds were at night
in the field in the starlight
when music loud and clear
sang from nowhere.

Will magic and the weeks placate
the soul that in tumbling fright
fled on August eighth?
The first flock is flying south

and a black-eyed susan
is livid in the autumn rain
dripping without haste or strain
on the oblong larger than a man.

Creator spirit come
by whom
I say that which is real
and softly away I steal.

Robert Hayden

Those Winter Sundays

Sundays too my father got up early
and put his clothes on in the blueblack cold,
then with cracked hands that ached
from labor in the weekday weather made
banked fires blaze. No one ever thanked him.

I'd wake and hear the cold splintering, breaking.
When the rooms were warm, he'd call,
and slowly I would rise and dress,
fearing the chronic angers of that house,

Speaking indifferently to him,
who had driven out the cold
and polished my good shoes as well.
What did I know, what did I know
of love's austere and lonely offices?

Delmore Schwartz

Father and Son

*"From a certain point onward there is no longer any
turning back. That is the point that must be reached."*
—Franz Kafka

Father:
On these occasions, the feelings surprise,
Spontaneous as rain, and they compel
Explicitness, embarrassed eyes—

Son:
Father, you're not Polonius, you're reticent,
But sure. I can already tell

The unction and falsetto of the sentiment
Which gratifies the facile mouth, but springs
From no felt, had, and wholly known things.

Father:
You must let me tell you what you fear
When you wake up from sleep, still drunk with sleep:
You are afraid of time and its slow drip,
Like melting ice, like smoke upon the air
In February's glittering sunny day.
Your guilt is nameless, because its name is time,
Because its name is death. But you can stop
Time as it dribbles from you, drop by drop.

Son:
But I thought time was full of promises,
Even as now, the emotion of going away—

Father:
That is the first of all its menaces,
The lure of a future different from today;
All of us always are turning away
To the cinema and Asia. All of us go
To one indeterminate nothing.

Son:
                                        Must it be so?
I question the sentiment you give to me,
As premature, not to be given, learned alone
When experience shrinks upon the chilling bone.
I would be sudden now and rash in joy,
As if I lived forever, the future my toy.
Time is a dancing fire at twenty-one,
Singing and shouting and drinking to the sun,
Powerful at the wheel of a motor-car,
Not thinking of death which is foreign and far.

Father:
If time flowed from your will and were a feast
I would be wrong to question your zest.
But each age betrays the same weak shape.
Each moment is dying. You will try to escape
From melting time and your dissipating soul
By hiding your head in a warm and dark hole.
See the evasions which so many don,
To flee the guilt of time they become one,
That is, the one number among masses,
The one anonymous in the audience,
The one expressionless in the subway,
In the subway evening among so many faces,
The one who reads the daily newspaper,
Separate from actor and act, a member
Of public opinion, never involved.
Integrated in the revery of a fine cigar,
Fleeing to childhood at the symphony concert,
Buying sleep at the drugstore, grandeur
At the band concert, Hawaii
On the screen, and everywhere a specious splendor:
One, when he is sad, has something to eat,
An ice cream soda, a toasted sandwich,
Or has his teeth fixed, but can always retreat
From the actual pain, and dream of the rich.
This is what one does, what one becomes
Because one is afraid to be alone,
Each with his own death in the lonely room.
But there is a stay. You can stop
Time as it dribbles from you, drop by drop.

Son:
Now I am afraid. What is there to be known?

Father:
Guilt, guilt of time, nameless guilt.
Grasp firmly your fear, thus grasping your self,

Your actual will. Stand in mastery,
Keeping time in you, its terrifying mystery.
Face yourself, constantly go back
To what you were, your own history.
You are always in debt. Do not forget
The dream postponed which would not quickly get
Pleasure immediate as drink, but takes
The travail of building, patience with means.
See the wart on your face and on your friend's face,
On your friend's face and indeed on your own face.
The loveliest woman sweats, the animal stains
The ideal which is with us like the sky . . . .

Son:
Because of that, some laugh, and others cry.

Father:
Do not look past and turn away your face.
You cannot depart and take another name,
Nor go to sleep with lies. Always the same,
Always the same self from the ashes of sleep
Returns with its memories, always, always,
The phoenix with eight hundred thousand memories!

Son:
What must I do that is most difficult?

Father:
You must meet your death face to face,
You must, like one in an old play,
Decide, once for all, your heart's place.
Love, power, and fame stand on an absolute
Under the formless night and the brilliant day,
The searching violin, the piercing flute.
Absolute! Venus and Caesar fade at that edge,
Hanging from the fiftieth story ledge,
Or diminished in bed when the nurse presses

Her sickening unguents and her cold compresses.
When the news is certain, surpassing fear,
You touch the wound, the priceless, the most dear.
There in death's shadow, you comprehend
The irreducible wish, world without end.

Son:
I begin to understand the reason for evasion,
I cannot partake of your difficult vision.

Father:
Begin to understand the first decision.
Hamlet is the example; only dying
Did he take up his manhood, the dead's burden,
Done with evasion, done with sighing,
Done with revery.
           Decide that you are dying
Because time is in you, ineluctable
As shadow, named by no syllable.
Act in that shadow, as if death were now:
Your own self acts then, then you know.

Son:
My father has taught me to be serious.

Father:
Be guilty of yourself in the full looking-glass.

Karl Shapiro

My Father's Funeral

Lurching from gloomy limousines we slip
On the warm baby-blanket of Baltimore snow,

Wet flakes smacking our faces like distraught
Kisses on cheeks, and step upon the green
Carpet of artificial grass which crunches
Underfoot, as if it were eating, and come
To the canopy, a half-shelter which provides
A kind of room to enclose us all, and the hole,
And the camp chairs, and following after,
The scrolly walnut coffin
That has my father in it.

Minutes ago in the noncommittal chapel
I saw his face, not looking himself at all
In that compartment hinged to open and shut,
A vaudeville prop with a small waxen man,
"So cold," the widow said and shied away
In a wide arc of centrifugal motion,
To come again to stand like me beside,
In the flowerless room with electric candelabra.
If there is among our people any heaven,
We are rather ambiguous about it
And tend to ignore the subject.

The rabbi's eulogy is succinct,
Accurate and sincere, and the great prayer
That finishes the speech is simply praise
Of God, the god my father took in stride
When he made us learn Hebrew and shorthand,
Taught us to be superior, as befits
A nation of individual priests.
At my sister's house we neither pray nor cry
Nor sit, but stand and drink and joke,
So that one of the youngsters says
It's more like a cocktail party.

For Dylan's dandy villanelle,
For Sylvia's oath of damnation one reserves
A technical respect. To Miller's Willie

And Lewis's Babbitt I demur.
My father was writing a book on salesmanship
While he was dying; it was his book of poems,
Destined to be unpublished. He hadn't time
To master books but kept the house well stocked
With random volumes, like a ship's library,
Rows and rows of forgotten classics,
Books for the sake of having books.

My father in black knee-socks and high shoes
Holding a whip to whip a top upstreet;
My father the court stenographer,
My father in slouch hat in the Rockies,
My father kissing my mother,
My father kissing his secretary,
In the high-school yearbook captioned Yid,
In synagogue at six in the morning praying
Three hundred and sixty-five days for his mother's rest,
My father at my elbow on the bimah
And presiding over the Sabbath.

In the old forgotten purlieus of the city
A Jewish ghetto in its day, there lie
My father's father, mother and the rest,
Now only a ghetto lost to time,
Ungreen, unwhite, unterraced like the new
Cemetery to which my father goes.
Abaddon, the old place of destruction;
Sheol, a new-made garden of the dead
Under the snow. Shalom be to his life,
Shalom be to his death.

David Ignatow

1. Brightness as a Poignant Light

I tread the dark and my steps are silent.
I am alone and feel a ghostly joy—wildly
free and yet I do not live absolutely
and forever, but my ghostly joy
is that I am come to light
for some reason known only to the dark,
perhaps to view itself in me.

As I tread the dark,
led by the light of my pulsating mind,
I am faithful to myself: my child.
Still, how can I be happy
to have been born only to return
to my father, the dark, to feel his power
and die?

I take comfort that I am
my father, speaking as a child
against my fatherhood. This
is the silence I hear my heart
beating in, but
not for me.

David Ignatow

A Requiem

My father listening to opera, that's me,
my legs stretched out upon the bed
as I lean back in my chair. I think of him

50

in his chair, legs crossed carelessly
and with his musing smile recalling his first wish,
to become a baritone, his smile seeking after his youth
or watching it in the distant past, untouchable.
I sat nearby feeling for him with love and sorrow
at his aging, the way I sit now,
with my writing as my only witness to my aging.
I am alone, and the opera playing heightens
my loneliness, without son, without father,
without past or present, and my future a problem.

      .   .   .   .

Eh, father, as I listen to your favorite opera
you would have enjoyed my listening and approved
emphatically, while I'd withhold myself,
tentative towards opera, as other matters burned in me,
such as the need to be free
and so we would argue but soon fall silent
and go our separate ways.

I am alone in my apartment, alone as you were
without me in your last days at about my age.
I am listening to Rossini and thinking of you
affectionately, longing for your presence once more,
of course to wrestle with your character,
the game once again of independence,
but now, now in good humour
because we already know the outcome,
for I am sixty-six, going on sixty-seven,
and you are forever seventy-two.
We are both old men and soon enough I'll join you,
so why quarrel again, as if two old men
could possibly settle between them
what was impossible to settle in their early days?

         *   *

David Ignatow

Father and Son

A black man is hugging me around the throat from behind with his forearm as he demands in a rapid undertone my money. I think of his embrace as nearly an affectionate one, as if from a son who has come up from behind to demand his stipend for the week in a playful imitation of a mugger. I turn carefully as I would to a son for whom I have the greatest affection and say gently, "The money is in my breast pocket," and I make a motion towards it with my hand. He strikes my hand, as if carrying on the game of mugger, in case, as in the game, I was reaching for a gun. I say again gently to my black son, "The wallet is in my breast pocket." He does not smile. He lets me reach into my jacket to bring forth the wallet, which I do, and he snatches it from me. The game between us has become serious. I am in danger, but I react with calm.

Is this my son, this tall, husky young man who is extracting the bills from the fold and now returning the wallet? I am cautious. I did not train him to be a killer nor threatener, but he is serious about the money, and he pockets it all. I have an empty wallet that I return automatically to my breast pocket. He and I look at each other. I think I have a smile on my face, and I think he sees it and is mildly astonished, and maybe understands it or is curious to see a smile. We look at each other for another moment. There is curiosity between us. This is not my son but another man's, and he is acting towards me as a stranger. We are strangers, but we are to each other in the relationship of father and son by age. He opens the door to the elevator and orders me in. Will he kill me in the elevator? I look into his face; he must realize what I am thinking. He holds open the door, waiting for me to enter, not threatening me, simply waiting, and I enter. The door closes behind me. I look through the porthole to see him looking back at me.

Is he taking a last look at the man who could be his father
whom he has subjugated to his will? I think I am still smiling.
I think he is smiling back as the elevator begins to climb.

John Berryman

Dream Songs

241

Father being the loneliest word in the one language
and a word only, a fraction of sun & guns
'way 'way ago,
on a hillside, under rain, maneuvers, once,
at big dawn. My field-glasses surpass—he sang—
yours.

Wicked & powerful, shy Henry   lifted his head with an
       offering.
Boots greeted him & it.
I raced into the bank,
my bank, after two years, with healthy cheques
& nobody seem to know me: was I ex-:
like Daddy??

O. O . . . I can't help feel I lift' the strain,
toward bottom. Games is somewhat too, but yet
certains improve
as if upon their only. We grinned wif wuv
for that which each of else was master of.
Christen the fallen.

384

The marker slants, flowerless, day's almost done,
I stand above my father's grave with rage,
often, often before
I've made this awful pilgrimage to one
who cannot visit me, who tore his page
out: I come back for more,

I spit upon this dreadful banker's grave
who shot his heart out in a Florida dawn
O ho alas alas
When will indifference come, I moan & rave
I'd like to scrabble till I got right down
away down under the grass

and ax the casket open ha to see
just how he's taking it, which he sought so hard
we'll tear apart
the mouldering grave clothes ha & then Henry
will heft the ax once more, his final card,
and fell it on the start.

Randall Jarrell

The Truth

When I was four my father went to Scotland.
They *said* he went to Scotland.

When I woke up I think I thought that I was dreaming—
I was so little then that I thought dreams
Are in the room with you, like the cinema.

That's why you don't dream when it's still light—
They pull the shades down when it is, so you can sleep.
I thought that then, but that's not right.
Really it's in your head.

And it was light then—light at *night*.
I heard Stalky bark outside.
But really it was Mother crying—
She coughed so hard she cried.
She kept shaking Sister,
She shook her and shook her.
I thought Sister had had her nightmare.
But he wasn't barking, he had died.
There was dirt all over Sister.
It was all streaks, like mud. I cried.
She didn't, but she was older.
                              I thought she didn't
Because she was older, I thought Stalky had just gone.
I got *everything* wrong.
I didn't get one single thing right.
It seems to me that I'd have thought
It didn't happen, like a dream,
Except that it was light. At night.
They burnt our house down, they burnt down London.
Next day my mother cried all day, and after that
She said to me when she would come to see me:
"Your father has gone away to Scotland.
He will be back after the war."

The war then was different from the war now.
The war now is *nothing*.

I used to live in London till they burnt it.
What was it like? It was just like here.
No, that's the truth.
My mother would come here, some, but she would cry.
She said to Miss Elise, "He's not himself";

She said, "Don't you love me any more at all?"
I was *my*self.
Finally she wouldn't come at all.
She never said one thing my father said, or Sister.
Sometimes she did,
Sometimes she was the same, but that was when I dreamed it.
I could tell I was dreaming, she was just the same.

That Christmas she bought me a toy dog.

I asked her what was its name, and when she didn't know
I asked her over, and when she didn't know
I said, "You're not my mother, you're not my mother.
She *hasn't* gone to Scotland, she is dead!"
And she said, "Yes, he's dead, he's dead!"
And cried and cried; she *was* my mother,
She put her arms around me and we cried.

William Stafford

My Father: October 1942

He picks up what he thinks is
a road map, and it is
his death: he holds it easily, and
nothing can take it from his firm hand.
The pulse in his thumb on the map
says, "1:19 P.M. next Tuesday, at
this intersection." And an ambulance
begins to throb while his face looks tired.

Any time anyone may pick up something
so right that he can't put it down:

that is the problem for all who travel—they
fatally own whatever is really theirs,
and that is the inner thread, the lock,
what can hold. If it is to be, nothing breaks
it. Millions of observers guess all the
time, but each person, once, can say, "Sure."

Then he's no longer an observer. He isn't right,
or wrong. He just wins or loses.

John Malcolm Brinnin

My Father, My Son

I

Father,
          one day longer on this earth than you,
I want you home—not
as a sage arthritic in red silks
to whom I proffer
                    birds of jade
& berries on a stick—not
as a totem with a spittled lip,
forked beard
              blown sidewise & Assyrian—
not as a democrat of rhetoric,
                                  calligraphy,
astride bowlegged Chippendale—but
just as the man you were
                          in dull Glen plaid,

high collar, homburg hat,
                             Kodak'd
beside our bathtub of a Hupmobile.
Your new estate is mine;
                             & if, at first,
I treat you like a well-scrubbed foreigner
to whom one gives a suit of clothes,
                                    five dollars
& a map of the city,
accept the circumstance: I need
help in the yard,
                    a hand with heavy things,
someone to keep the books.

II

Flames I've not eaten
                    I have quashed
with a small cap of silver—yet
what was it like when,
                        clacking west,
you heard the waters hiss & part,
                                & saw
the sun rise cold as cash?
                        Your eyes
like plums in fifty watts
                        of washroom light,
you shaved, halfway across Ontario,
with a straight razor & your braces down.
Bandbox fresh,
                whisked to your high-topped shoes,
when you stepped from a Grand Trunk sleeping car,
what was it like to be,
                        emblazoned in your tracks,
one man alive,
                Gladstone in hand?

Those boom-town dollar bills—were they
not barbarous as they were absurd?
When, Sunday afternoons,
                              they showered
out of canvas biplanes onto
                                   lots for sale,
& craven girls, knee-deep
in goldenrod & Queen Anne's lace,
picked them like lettuce,
                              was not history,
finally, a subdivision of brown bungalows,
                                        a small
down payment on the Middle West,
& good clean fun?
                    On the Tashmoo boat,
its splashy paddle wheels
                              walking the water,
did I not watch
                 the snake dance
                                   deck to deck
of realtor & typist,
                    branch manager & clerk?
Your hands outstretched,
                              your fingertips upon
a boozy woman's pin-striped back,
                                   two other
hands on yours,
                 et cetera—*Yes!* you sang,
your flint face mesmerized,
                              Yes!
we have no bananas,
we have no *bananas today!*

III

Set down in our raw suburb
                              Mother wept,

59

her old life now a province in a mist
where military bands,
                        caged in an iron wedding cake,
played Humperdinck & Grieg
                        to the King's swans;
& years of calling cards,
                        laid in a silver dish,
tallied the last turns in the vestibule
of waltzing osprey & high-stepping fox.
                                    You must
have understood,
                    though you would not,
the vast leer of our Morris chair,
the desolations of Caruso on the console,
                                    the ache
of Maxfield Parrish's blue dawn
above a five-foot shelf of books,
                            glassed in.
Why was she crying?
Where did she hurt?
                    Shrunk in the threat
of something still more awful
                        than the oven eyes
of grizzlies,
            chained,
                    snarling, to a pole,
that wanted to get at me,
                        I lay, eyes shut, awake.
"He's not asleep."
                Her sob
broke like a bubble on a pink geranium.
"He's a good actor. Jack, see what you can do."
Shoshonis gobbling at the sight of him,
                                    Buffalo Bill,
that worn-out hero of your one-man repertoire,

skirmished across my bed.
                              What a brute!
I think you thought so too.

IV

Father,
        what do I do with years
still hovering like a castle quarried to its floors,
wrapped,
            piece by piece in burlap,
                              stacked away
in some red warehouse just outside of town?
To whom can I show off?
                        Where now can I talk big?
Blood on my hockey stick,
                        I limped home
pitifully.
        Marbles in my mouth,
I got my message through to Garcia,
                              & stalked
the dining room for liberty or death.
Erasmus redivivus,
I fell asleep in the encyclopedia.
                        When you
told your one joke
                (Irate Diner: Waitress—what is
this fly doing in my soup?
                        Waitress: Why—it does look like
the breaststroke, sir.)
                I laughed
louder than anyone. I said
your Friday haircut was the cat's pajamas.
I said
        So's *your old man!*
                & bit my tongue.

You pondered *The Outline of History,*
                                        you took up golf.
I sulked & fasted,
                told my beads,
                                slammed
out to Mass at dawn.
                        The simplest form
of tyranny, I learned,
                        is holiness.
Remember our most delicate of interviews?
I had to know what it was all about;
                                        you had to say.
My eyes outstaring yours—
                        yours fixed,
first on my saints, all smiles in their blue lights,
then on my 2 for 25¢ photographs
                        of Bebe Daniels & Ben Lyon,
then on the water-falling tails
                        of birds of paradise
you'd painted on my walls—
                        you began
at the beginning, you told it all.
                                Hushed
by great news, I sat stock-still as,
                                surfacing
from 20,000 leagues,
                you lit a Camel
& then studied it. "Do you think you understand?"
I nodded,
        completely in the dark.
                                That's where I stayed
until,
        one morning in a field,
                                instructed
by a playmate grown up fast,

I thought my head, like a boiled egg,
was sliced off at the top.

V

You couldn't bear it,
                          yet every June
you'd pack us off, dolls in a box,
to summer in the Maritimes.
                          "Hon,"
you wrote from the East Side Y.M.C.A.,
"I don't think I can stand it.
                          I eat
at some dog wagon near the office,
read *Liberty,* take in a show."

Stalled like a whale,
                          her hawsers loose,
the S.S. Berengaria
lay sidling at the Ocean Terminal.
                          At noon,
her deck rails lined with duchesses,
she churned the harbor skidding in her bells,
then dropped her tugs
                          & slid
basso profundo out to sea.

                          I still
had graves to dig:
                          a cricket skewered on a pin,
a grasshopper dismantled to its knees.
I put them
            side by side,
                          a few
limp dandelions for one,
purple clover for the other,

                                       a matchstick
cross for each. I had no sympathy.

                           VI

Up in the smoke of 1929 went your big deal.
Grass withered in the cleats
                              of your golf shoes.
You closed the office,
                          hocked your turnip watch,
replaced the lining in your overcoat.
Across a neighborhood of rotting mortgages
you saw your future out of sight.
They even tried to repossess the car!
Thank God,
               you still had brushes & a union card.
You climbed a ladder,
                          you began to paint
a painted desert, streets in Trinidad,
a salmon-colored *auberge* in a forest where,

descending,
               weightless,
                              from a tulip coach,
Lucrezia Bori,
                 like a walking tent,
embraced the full measure of illicit joy.
                                          Back
in overalls, you made good money
                                    & you grew morose.
What could you do with a kid afraid of heights,
half-crocked on Proust,
                          tooling a sonnet
on the very day the Tigers clinched the pennant?

VII

Father,
          riddle me this:
                    If I'm not half
the man you were,
                    what fortune makes you
all I am?
You gave me your car keys.
I put you on the shelf.
                    What did you know
of Tzara, Aschenbach, Barbusse?
How could you stomach Hitler & Republic Steel?
Out all night,
          my fingers mimeo'd
with U.A.W. strike bulletins,
I made the breakfast nook my drumhead court.
Charged with murder,
                    you sat still.
Hectored out of conscience, you,
with crypto-fascist nonchalance,
                              ate two
fried eggs,
          a slice of ham,
                    & dolloped
cream into your coffee. You had to see a man,
you said, about a dog,
                    then wiped your lips
& handed me a week's allowance.

VIII

Cranking a winch one working day,
                    your hands went white.

A stippled garden shuddered to the stage.
So much to say,
                    I couldn't get there fast enough.

Time eats you in that box I bought
next morning in a sort of catacomb
on Jefferson near East Grand Boulevard.

Tailgating your black Packard to Mount Olivet,
lights on,
              we ran the lights,
                          stopped dead
in a charred grove &,
                    ill at ease,
                              stood witness
to your last embarrassment.
                          Traffic with insane
persistence scratched the hedges.
                          Overhead,
like pterodactyls sitting on the wind,
Ford Tri-Motors snored importantly
                              & side-slipped home.
Broken at the wrist,
                  the hand you never shook
hung at my side.
                  I can't remember—
did the rain hold off?

In your collar box I found
                      love poems—
Love poems! When had you written them? To whom?
Your heart, you said, it "burned,"
                              it "yearned."
You said, "You make the winter rains seem glad, my dear.
          The sky above me smiles when you are near."

They were so bad I cried.

John Ciardi

Elegy

My father was born with a spade in his hand and traded it
for a needle's eye to sit his days cross-legged on tables
till he could sit no more, then sold insurance, reading
the ten-cent-a-week lives like logarithms from
the Tables of Metropolitan to their prepaid tombstones.

Years of the little dimes twinkling on kitchen tables
at Mrs. Fauci's at Mrs. Locatelli's at Mrs. Cataldo's
(*Arrividerla, signora. A la settimana prossima. Mi saluta,
la prego, il marito, Ciao, Anna. Bye-bye.*)
—known as a Debit. And with his ten-year button

he opened a long dream like a piggy bank, spilling the dimes
like mountain water into the moss of himself, and bought
ten piney lots in Wilmington. Sunday by Sunday
he took the train to his woods and walked under the trees
to leave his print on his own land, a patron of seasons.

I have done nothing as perfect as my father's Sundays
on his useless lots. Gardens he dreamed from briar tangle
and the swampy back slope of his ridge rose over him
more flowering than Brazil. Maples transformed to figs,
and briar to blood-blue grapes in his look around

when he sat on a stone with his wine-jug and cheese beside him,
his collar and coat on a branch, his shirt open,
his derby back on his head like a standing turtle. A big
man he was. When he sang *Celeste Aida* the woods
filled as if a breeze were swelling through them.

When he stopped, I thought I could hear the sound still moving.
—Well, I have lied. Not so much lied as dreamed it.
I was three when he died. It was someone else—my sister—
went with him under the trees. But if it was her
memory then, it became mine so long since

I will owe nothing on it, having dreamed it from all
the nights I was growing, the wet-pants man of the family.
I have done nothing as perfect as I have dreamed him
from old-wives tales and the running of my blood.
God knows what queer long darks I had no eyes for

followed his stairwell weeks to his Sunday breezeways.
But I will swear the world is not well made that rips
such gardens from the week. Or I should have walked
a saint's way to the cross and nail by nail
hymned out my blood to glory, for one good reason.

Theodore Weiss

The death of fathers

Rummaging inside yourself
for clues and coming up
with nothing more than old
familiar news, you think
you have it hard.
                    Your
father having died when you
were still a child, you keep,
it's true, but faded sense
of him.
          Nearly as bad,
not long after that
the village he was born
and lived in all his life
dispersed.
              And now, as if

it joined, he with it,
the lost tribes of Virginia,
it exists, name only,
on discarded maps.
            And you
blame blustering Pittsburgh,
the smoke of it, the noise
its days cannot contain,
the ruin these suggest.

But though my father died
when I was some years older,
I know, beyond all ordinary
disappearings, nothing
of his past, his country

(Hungary he called it,
a few oaths still peppery
on my tongue what's left
to prove it), least of all
his town.
            New vandals
rampant, kicking boundaries
about, whole nations on
the run, as though their
lands were made of wind-

blown sand, how expect
to know? Like you I try
to ferret out some hints
of him from the one source
still available—myself.

Recall a few of his
loved saws like "The apple
falls not far from its tree."
But only a worm sticks
its fat tongue out at me.

Or "Teddy, I understand
you all right. Are you not
my son?" Well, was he not
my father? Clues or not,
I plunge into my writing,

chase fast scribbled
line on line, lean hard
on his robustious love:
his skill with animals:
his pleasure in the violin

he played by ear, gypsy
gaiety, abandon, gathered
up like grapes ripening
within his fingers' will:
his passion for his work,

my awe at watching him
delight in old things, new,
he bought to sell, green
cabinets he danced among,
as he, a young boy still,

shoes astride his neck,
had skipped along (he told
me this?) the dappled path
through the Black Forest:
pride that almost drove

him, raging, over cliffs
and finally, when he would,
despite strong warnings,
mount a frisky horse, rode
him off forever,
                    I there
as he stumbles up, eyes
closed, face set, the iron

bar lying just behind him
for what it's done
                    moved
little farther than before,
a last cry, mother's name,
still hot upon his lips.
He staggered about,

I, gripping his arm,
summon all my strength
("Am I not your son?"
Surely I can reach him,
haul him back) to learn—

as I shout "Father!"
over the growing chasm,
his breath slammed to,
an instant wall erected—
the fundamental lesson.

Robert Lowell

Father

There was rebellion, Father, and the door was slammed.
Front doors were safe with glass then ... you fell backward
on your heirloom-clock, the phases of the moon,
the highboy quaking to its toes. My Father ...
I haven't lost heart to say *I knocked you down.* ...
I have breathed the seclusion of the life-tight den,
card laid on card until the pack is used,
old Helios turning the houseplants to blondes,

moondust blowing in the prowling eye—
a parental sentence on each step misplaced....
You were further from Death than I am now—
that Student ageless in her green cloud of hash,
her bed a mattress half a foot off floor...
as far from us as her young breasts will stretch.

Robert Lowell

Commander Lowell

1887-1950

There were no undesirables or girls in my set,
when I was a boy at Mattapoisett—
only Mother, still her Father's daughter.
Her voice was still electric
with a hysterical, unmarried panic,
when she read to me from the Napoleon book.
Long-nosed Marie Louise
Hapsburg in the frontispiece
had a downright Boston bashfulness,
where she grovelled to Bonaparte, who scratched his navel,
and bolted his food—just my seven years tall!
And I, bristling and manic,
skulked in the attic,
and got two hundred French generals by name,
from *A* to *V*—from Augereau to Vandamme.
I used to dope myself asleep,
naming those unpronounceables like sheep.

Having a naval officer
for my Father was nothing to shout
about to the summer colony at "Matt."
He wasn't at all "serious,"
when he showed up on the golf course,
wearing a blue serge jacket and numbly cut
white ducks he'd bought
at a Pearl Harbor commissariat....
and took four shots with his putter to sink his putt.
"Bob," they said, "golf's a game you really ought to know
      how to play,
if you play at all."
They wrote him off as "naval,"
naturally supposed his sport was sailing.
Poor Father, his training was engineering!
Cheerful and cowed
among the seadogs at the Sunday yacht club,
he was never one of the crowd.
"Anchors aweigh," Daddy boomed in his bathtub,
"Anchors aweigh,"
when Lever Brothers offered to pay
him double what the Navy paid.
I nagged for his dress sword with gold braid,
and cringed because Mother, new
caps on all her teeth, was born anew
at forty. With seamanlike celerity,
Father left the Navy,
and deeded Mother his property.

He was soon fired. Year after year,
he still hummed "Anchors aweigh" in the tub—
whenever he left a job,
he bought a smarter car.
Father's last employer
was Scudder, Stevens and Clark, Investment Advisors,
himself his only client.

While Mother dragged to bed alone,
read Menninger,
and grew more and more suspicious,
he grew defiant.
Night after night,
à la clarté déserte de sa lampe,
he slid his ivory Annapolis slide rule
across a pad of graphs—
piker speculation! In three years
he squandered sixty thousand dollars.

Smiling on all,
Father was once successful enough to be lost
in the mob of ruling-class Bostonians.
As early as 1928,
he owned a house converted to oil,
and redecorated by the architect
of St. Mark's School.... Its main effect
was a drawing room, "longitudinal as Versailles,"
its ceiling, roughened with oatmeal, was blue as the sea.
And once
nineteen, the youngest ensign in his class,
he was "the old man" of a gunboat on the Yangtze.

Robert Lowell

Sheridan

Another day of standstill heat,
old American summer, Old Glory,
only the squeaking, floppy lapwings
and garrulous foreign colony of jackdaws

are English, all else is American.
Placed chestnut trees flower mid-cowfield,
even in harvest time, they swear,
"We always had leaves and ever shall."

Sheridan, you gleam and stall in the heat,
mislaying as many things as people;
your whole plastic armory, claymore,
Nazi helmet, batwings, is lost.
But who would hide weapons that do
everything true weapons should, but hurt?
"You're Mr. Loser," you say, "you lost our guns."
You say it in Kentish cockney: *weir* guns.

How unretentive we become,
yet weirdly naked like you. Today
only the eternal midday separates
you from our unchangeably sunset
and liver-invigorated faces. High-hung,
the period scythe silvers in the sun,
a cutting edge, a bounding line,
between the child's world and the earth—

Our early discovery that only children grow.

Gil Orlovitz

Art of the Sonnet: XXXIII

If I could rise and see my father young,
with horse and Torah in the Russian town,
sugar might tremble on my tongue,
and Jehovah roar as I tumble Him down.

If I could rise and see my father sweet
and stern, as boys endure a boyhood dream
only to surrender secretly,
love's espionage I could memorize
knowing I have his youth before he dies.
I could at last allow the man his age
without the stupefying lamentations
that must have him obsolete before assuage,
that this sweet epitaph dissolve upon my tongue:
Thus my father—Living old, died young.

William Jay Smith

American Primitive

Look at him there in his stovepipe hat,
His high-top shoes, and his handsome collar;
Only my Daddy could look like that,
And I love my Daddy like he loves his Dollar.

The screen door bangs, and it sounds so funny—
There he is in a shower of gold;
His pockets are stuffed with folding money,
His lips are blue, and his hands feel cold.

He hangs in the hall by his black cravat,
The ladies faint, and the children holler:
Only my Daddy could look like that,
And I love my Daddy like he loves his Dollar.

Irving Wexler

Elegy for My Father
(Part VIII)

When Friday nights are lucky, you
shout us to the kitchen table,
the smell of work still clinging
to your waiter's jacket. Lavishly,
you pour your tips, your only wages,
between the polished candlesticks.
My sisters and I, giddy with the riches,
build the coins into magic towers.
Under the flicker of Sabbath flames,
the nickels, dimes and quarters,
a once-in-a-bluemoon silver dollar,
glimmer like antique gold. "You win,"
you shout, sliding three quarters
toward us on the damask, like a croupier.
Laughing, you press the precious
coins one on each forehead.
Lean Fridays, when the money towers
are low, you grimly urge buffalo
nickels into our reluctant palms,
push your meager harvest toward the folds
of Mama's silence. An ache for you
as desolate as the space between us,
we watch you, lovelorn, reading The Forward,
your frogeyes looming hugely helpless
behind a heavy magnifying glass,
like some pathetic monster out of
a comic-strip fairy tale.
Suddenly a shame, a fear, a pity
is among us. What shall we do,
offer a sign of love? Hold our tongues?

In the bedroom, Mama's feet are furious
birds winging the treadle of her
Singer sewing machine.

Robert Duncan

A Set of Romantic Hymns
(Part II)

Fountain of forms! Life springs of unique being!

Never again this sequence I am.
Never again this one hand
    drawing its song from men's words.

Never again this one life, this
    universe bent to this lyre
    he would make in the language
            for music's sake.

Never again just this derivation
    from manhood, these numbers,
    this dwelling in the shape of things.

        My Father flies upon the air,
        shakes down black night around me,
        for where I think of him
        his wings are there, his
        crownd eye, his horny beak,
            his lingering cry.

        And from the thought of him I go
        out of all human shape into that pain,
        that crows-skin wizard likeness

ravaging man most is,
    having a hand in the claw's work,
the outraging talon
    scraping the hare's bone.

Pure Omen! under the storm cloud

he becomes a bird of the storm.

Burning in the blaze he flies!

Howard Nemerov

To David, about His Education

The world is full of mostly invisible things,
And there is no way but putting the mind's eye,
Or its nose, in a book, to find them out,
Things like the square root of Everest
Or how many times Bryon goes into Texas,
Or whether the law of the excluded middle
Applies west of the Rockies. For these
And the like reasons, you have to go to school
And study books and listen to what you are told,
And sometimes try to remember. Though I don't know
What you will do with the mean annual rainfall
On Plato's *Republic*, or the calorie content
Of the *Diet of Worms*, such things are said to be
Good for you, and you will have to learn them
In order to become one of the grown-ups
Who sees invisible things neither steadily nor whole,
But keeps gravely the grand confusion of the world
Under his hat, which is where it belongs,
And teaches small children to do this in their turn.

Hayden Carruth

My Father's Face

Old he was but not yet wax,
old and old but not yet gray.
What an awkwardness of facts
gray and waxen when he lay.

Rage had held me forty years,
only five have sought his grace.
Will my disproportionate tears
quell at last his smiling face?

Awkwardly at his behest
I this queer rhyme try to make
after one that he loved best,
made long since by Willy Blake.

       *   *   *

Cannot. In
my own way, half inarticulate,
must sing the blues.

Oh how he lay there
quiet as cast dice, crooked. They had given him
a face he never wore

smiling like anyone,
like God—
he, my own, who had smiled only

in the smear of pain,
as now my hemlock smears in this wind
dripping with half-snow, half-rain.

Smoke flares from my stovepipe,
breaks sharply down, away,
blue, whipping the leafless alders, vanishing,

80

while I watch from my window, this shack
in a scrap of meadow
going to woods—

alder, chokecherry, yellow birch, ash,
and the one old hemlock leaning forth,
smeared in half-snow, half-rain, November and the north.

*   *   *

Southward, downcountry
was where he lay
and I stood

in a loathsome mass of bleeding flowers
that April. Sun flashed and was gone, cold.
We two there, lashed stiff in old antagonism,

yet altered. It was that new smile
fingered on him, official, patented,
like the oil that shone on the pale oak catafalque:

such means they use to publicize, to promote
a marketable death.
He was worthy, worthy!—

I blurted, tried to blurt
in the clench of a surprise of tears.
And then my anger shifted from him to them.

In that horror
of hurting flowers
where I stood and he lay

I, frozen, was turned around inside my years
as a shadow turns
inside the changing day.

*   *   *

81

Why couldn't they let him be himself?
Like all our family he smiled
with a downturned mouth.

No doubt professional death-tenders are required,
competence is required, yet I wish they had let him
lie as he had fallen,

old Darwinist smiling
at the light gone down in the south,
at the leaf gone down.

Strangely, the birds had come. Already
in cold twilight robins sang,
and he heard them, the simple but rich song,

like Blake's, melodious for a fair season to come,
he heard them and he fell down,
unable to last till summer.

It was a reversal.
At the wrong time, in April, light dwindled
and the leaf fell down.

But hearts burst any time.
He took it smiling
with a downturned mouth.

                    *   *   *

The old Socialist!
And his father before him.
Era of eyeshades, rolltops, late tracks in a snowy street,

a flare of shots maybe in the dark,
and the talk, talk: that man eating,
this man not.

It was all so blessedly simple.
Hate, hate the monopolists!
Ah, and have I not, sirrah?—

but power of money has bought the power of heart,
monopoly eats the word, eats thought, desire,
your old companions now in the thick of it, eating—

is that betrayal? They fatten, but for my part
old hatred deepens,
deepening as monopoly deepens,

until my socialism has driven me to the sociality
of trees, snow, rocks, the north—solitude.
Strange outcome. Like so many.

I'll walk now; the woody meadow,
the firs, the brook, then higher to the birches.
I wish you were coming too.

        *   *   *

"Alyosha left his father's house
feeling more depressed and
crushed in spirit

than when he entered it..." I walk,
going at last nowhere
in the snow and rain

that lock in air
and nap the gray rock with gray fur.
Beside me, among the ferns that confide

their green trust to the snow,
something stalks, or seems to stalk. A partridge?
Or my mind's shadow? Minute fires flow

in the lichened rock, and a yellow eye
blinks like a shuttered lens among the ferns.
Shadows and strange fires,

who can deny them, aspects of the cold world
and the father's house? We rebel
backward, ever backward, going

behind the ancestral impositions of reality.
To seek, to find—not to impose. So we say.
But it is a sad business.

*   *   *

Once he brought
to his blue house in the guttering chestnut forest—
oh, I remember this—

a pomegranate in his pocket.
But let me describe to you a killed chestnut tree.
Leaves, fruit, even the bark have long fallen

to the dark alien disease, and at last
the tree itself lies down
in a twisted, rising-and-falling

shape, and it never rots.
The smooth wood, pale and intense,
undulates

in a kind of serpentine passivity
among waves of witch hazel and dogwood
that wash along it

summer after summer after summer.
And so the killed chestnut has become
something everlasting in the woods,

like Yggdrasill. Tradition is not convention.

Tradition is always unexpected,
like the taste of the pomegranate, so sweet.

                *   *   *

I must complete my turning.
With purpose, very coolly, I raise my vision,
snipping

a thread of the net that holds
everything together.
My splashing fears subside about my knees.

How easy! I wonder why
I took so long, learning
that to destroy

what could never be either right or wrong,
this net, this mere order
or any order,

is no real destruction—
look, I walk as I have always walked,
one foot in front of the other foot.

The rocks and birches take so warmly
to the purity of their restoration. I see this.
I have done it with one gesture, like that.

I walk in the tact of the ultimate rebel
graduated from conspiracy,
free, truly free, in the wonder of uncreation.

                *   *   *

Well, the traditions of woods are sweet,
but something is withheld, something...
O my father, where is the real monopolist?

Can I, alien, avoid spreading
my dark disease? But you would say then,
seek its purity, deep at the root, radically.

If the orderly massacre of order creates an order,
then let it be new, even now, from the beginnings of things.
I am cold to my bones, my red hand clings

like a wind-plastered leaf to a white bole of birch,
the sky is speckled with snow-flecks
driven downwind, vanishing. It is all a song

vanishing down the wind, like snow,
like the last leaves of the birch
spinning away in harsh beauty. The hardhack,

clotted with snow, bends and rattles,
a sound like jeering in the driven twilight.
Why must the song be so intricate? What am I now,

what is my sorrow, has it not spun away?
Your face, snow-flecked, seems torn
downwind like the song of birch leaves.

*   *   *

Confused darkness turns a page. Wind slackens,
cold night is beginning, in the last light
the god of winter walks, gray and alone,

Odin, Windigo, St. Malachy, someone
with a downturned smile brushing the fir boughs,
shaking the dead reeds and ferns.

Snow thickens, leaning toward the south.
Could he come home tonight
to his house, his woods, the snow, the snow-light?

My thought sings into snow, vanishing.

At least I have two clear choices: to stamp
in deepening cold, half-blind, dragging

my feet in freezing ferns, determining
my way in darkness, to the ragged meadow,
the shack with the rusty stove;

or to stay where I am in the rustle of snow
while my beard clots and whitens
and the world recedes into old purity

and the snow opens at last to the stars
that will glisten like silent histories breaking
over a silent face, smiling and cold.

*　　　*　　　*

O thou quiet northern snow
reaching southward wave on wave,
southward to the land below,
billow gently on his grave.

Snowy owl that glides alone,
softly go, defend his rest;
buntings, whirl around his stone
softly, thou the wintriest.

Gently, softly, o my kind,
snow and wind and driven leaf,
take him, teach my rebel mind
trust at last in this cold grief.

Hayden Carruth

The Smallish Son

A small voice is fretting my house in the night,
a small heart is there . . .
                              Listen,
I who have dwelt at the root of a scream forever,
I who have read my heart like a man with no hands
reading a book whose pages turn in the wind,
I say listen, listen, hear me
in our dreamless dark, my dear. I can teach you complaining.
My father, being wise, knowing the best rebellion is at forty,
told me to wait; but when he was sixty
he had nothing to say. Then do not wait.
Could I too not tell you much of a young man's folly?
But you will learn. When you play at strife-of-the-eyes
with existence, staring at the fluorescent moon to see
which of you will go under, please, please
be the first to smile. Do not harden yourself
though it means surrendering all, turning yourself out
to be known at the world's mercy. You will lose your name,
you will not know the curious shape of your coat,
even the words you breathe, spoken out so clearly,
will loosen and disperse forever, all given over
to the wind crying upon distant seas. Moment of horror:
the moonlight will name you, a profile among fallen flowers.
Yet you may survive, for many have done so. You need
only to close your eyes, beautiful feminine gesture;
and do not be afraid of the strange woman you find
lying in the chamber of your throat. When a silver bird
strikes at the shutters of your eyes with his wings
admit him, do not attempt to tame him, but as he swoops
in the tall glimmer of your intricate room
admire his freedom; and when a silver mouse
scurries twittering through the passageways of your blood
consider his beauty. So it will be: dark, a long vigil,

far among splendors of despair, this creation
in the closed eye. Everything will be true, pure,
your love most of all, and your flesh in the drunkenness
of becoming a dream. Lingering among the revenants
who still bear your name, touching and kissing,
dancing among their tatters of skin and splintered bones,
noticing the song of the tomb, how it soars in dream,
you in your sovereignty condescending to song,
permitting your myth— what awareness then, what ecstasies
in the shimmering dark pool, what marvels of the dark stair!
But now, please open your eyes again. Have we not said
down with all tyrants, even our own? Especially our own!
Open your eyes; they will glitter from long sleep
with the knowledge of the other side of the world.
Their light then will be of such a quiet intensity
that smiles and frowns will fall away like shadows
of wild birds flying over. No complicity, no acquiescence;
and yet a degree of affection remaining, as when one finds
an old bible in an old cupboard of an empty house.
So it is, so, freedom and beauty. Do not be modest,
wear the delicate beauty of those crippled at birth
who earn the grace of their maiming. Do not be afraid,
assume the freedom of those born in their captivity
who earn the purity of their being. All one and all many,
but remember, never the two alone, falsely dividing
in the mind's paralyzed divorce. This is our meaning
under our true rebellion, this is the dark where we
may venture without our dreams. In the dreamless dark
where I await you, the dark light of my eyes
may still be darkly burning when you come.
You must look and you must seek
for my eyes will answer but I think they will not summon.
And if you do not find them, turn away.

Hayden Carruth

The Little Fire in the Woods

Even these stones I placed crudely once,
black now from many fires, bring me
a little knowledge, things I've done,
times endured, saying I am this one, this
person, as night falls through the trees. I see sand
darkening by the edge of an ocean, lights
on the rim of a galaxy, but I have not planned

my visions. I wish I could. We used birch bark
and spruce cones for tinder tonight, in which
a spark rambled until it met itself, flaring then
and leaping, throwing shadows among the trees.
Now punky gray birch smolders. Held
in the roots of our great spruce, I hold
my son, and the darkness thickens. It isn't

the cares of day I think of any longer.
True, I got this bruised belly when the machine
kicked this afternoon in our troubled potato patch
where the earth too cried out for justice,
justice! I tauten my muscles; the pain
is good and I wish it could be everything. But
larger errors are what we think of now

that have flared and leapt and thrown these shadows
of extinction among our objects. Or is the error
necessity, a circle closing? Son, in nature all
successions end. How long and slow is chaos.
Anywhere I am I see the slow surge of fire—
I, a diffraction, nothing. My son moves
closer. "Pop, how does the fire make heat?"

He does not see the fire I see, but I know
he knows a terror that children have never
known before, waiting for him. He knows.

Our love is here, this night, these woods, existing;
it is now. I think how its being
must emanate, like heat in conversion,
out beyond the woods to the stars, and how

it joins there in the total reckoning. It *must*.
Could anyone resist this longing all the time?
Oh, I know what I know, and I cannot
unknow it, crying out too for justice,
while the fire dwindles and shadows rise and flow.
But listen, something is here in the forest. Listen.
It is very clear and it whispers a little song:

> Sweet Bo I know thee
> 		thou art ten
> and knowest now thy father is
> five times more again
> 			and more
> and most gone out of rhymes
> sweet Bo
> 		for thou dost know me
>
> And thou old spruce above us
> many are they of comrade and kin
> who love us
> 			so that their loving proveth
> everything
> 			although their way hath not
> the same compassion
> 			as thy nonloving.
>
> Sweet Bo good night and hold me
> hold me close
> 			the good firelight
> is dying
> 		the woods are sighing

                    and great is the dark
                                        grateful
            am I for thee sweet Bo
                                    good night
            good night.

Richard Wilbur

My Father Paints the Summer

A smoky rain riddles the ocean plains,
Rings on the beaches' stones, stomps in the swales,
Batters the panes
Of the shore hotel, and the hoped-for summer chills and
    fails.
The summer people sigh,
"Is this July?"

They talk by the lobby fire but no one hears
For the thrum of the rain. In the dim and sounding halls,
Din at the ears,
Dark at the eyes well in the head, and the ping-pong balls
Scatter their hollow knocks
Like crazy clocks.

But up in his room by artificial light
My father paints the summer, and his brush
Tricks into sight
The prosperous sleep, the girdling stir and clear steep hush
Of a summer never seen,
A granted green.

Summer, luxuriant Sahara, the orchard spray
Gales in the Eden trees, the knight again
Can cast away
His burning mail, Rome is at Anzio: but the rain
For the ping-pong's optative bop
Will never stop.

Caught Summer is always an imagined time.
Time gave it, yes, but time out of any mind.
There must be prime
In the heart to beget that season, to reach past rain and find
Riding the palest days
Its perfect blaze.

Howard Moss

Elegy for My Father

Father, whom I murdered every night but one,
That one, when your death murdered me,
Your body waits within the wasting sod.
Clutching at the straw-face of your God,
Do you remember me, your morbid son,
Curled in a death, all motive unbegun,
Continuum of flesh, who never thought to be
The mourning mirror of your potency?

All you had battled for the nightmare took
Away, as dropping from your eyes, the sea-
Salt tears, with messages that none could read,
Impotent, pellucid, were the final seeds
You sowed. Above you, the white night nurse shook

His head, and, moaning on the moods of luck,
We knew the double-dealing enemy:
From pain you suffered, pain had set you free.

Down from the ceiling, father, circles came:
Angels, perhaps, to bear your soul away.
But tasting the persisting salt of pain,
I think my tears created them, though, in vain,
Like yours, they fell. All losses link: the same
Creature marred us both to stake his claim.
Shutting my eyelids, barring night and day,
I saw, and see, your body borne away.

Two months dead, I wrestle with your name
Whose separate letters make a paltry sum
That is not you. If still you harbor mine,
Think of the house we had in summertime
When in the sea-light every early game
Was played with love and, if death's waters came,
You'd rescue me. How I would take you from,
Now, if I could, its whirling vacuum.

(1955)

James Dickey

The Hospital Window

I have just come down from my father.
Higher and higher he lies
Above me in a blue light
Shed by a tinted window.
I drop through six white floors
And then step out onto pavement.

Still feeling my father ascend,
I start to cross the firm street,
My shoulder blades shining with all
The glass the huge building can raise.
Now I must turn round and face it,
And know his one pane from the others.

Each window possesses the sun
As though it burned there on a wick.
I wave, like a man catching fire.
All the deep-dyed windowpanes flash,
And, behind them, all the white rooms
They turn to the color of Heaven.

Ceremoniously, gravely, and weakly,
Dozens of pale hands are waving
Back, from inside their flames.
Yet one pure pane among these
Is the bright, erased blankness of nothing.
I know that my father is there,

In the shape of his death still living.
The traffic increases around me
Like a madness called down on my head.
The horns blast at me like shotguns,
And drivers lean out, driven crazy—
But now my propped-up father

Lifts his arm out of stillness at last.
The light from the window strikes me
And I turn as blue as a soul,
As the moment when I was born.
I am not afraid for my father—
Look! He is grinning; he is not

Afraid for my life, either,
As the wild engines stand at my knees
Shredding their gears and roaring,

And I hold each car in its place
For miles, inciting its horn
To blow down the walls of the world

That the dying may float without fear
In the bold blue gaze of my father.
Slowly I move to the sidewalk
With my pin-tingling hand half dead
At the end of my bloodless arm.
I carry it off in amazement,

High, still higher, still waving,
My recognized face fully mortal,
Yet not; not at all, in the pale,
Drained, otherworldly, stricken,
Created hue of stained glass.
I have just come down from my father.

James Dickey

To His Children in Darkness

You hear my step
Come close, and stop.
I shut the door.
By the two-deck bed
And its breathing sheets
Houselight is killed
From off my breast.
I am unseen,
But sensed, but known,
And now begin

To be what I
Can never be,
But what I am
Within your dream:
A god or beast
Come true at last.
To one, I have
Like leaves grown here.
And furl my wings
As poplars sigh.

And slowly let
On him a breath
Drawn in a cloud,
In which he sees
Angelic hosts
Like blowing trees
Send me to earth
To root among
The secret soil
Of his dark room.

The other hears
A creature shed
Throughout the maze
The same long breath
As he conceives
That he no more
Desires to live
In blazing sun,
Nor shake to death
The animal

Of his own head.
I know what lies
Behind all words.
Like a beast, mismade,

Which finds its brain
Can sing alone
Without a sound
At what he is
And cannot change,
Or like a god

Which slowly breathes
Eternal life
Upon a soul
In deepest sleep.
My heart's one move
Comes now, and now.
A god strikes root
On touching earth.
A beast can hold
The thought of self

Between his horns
Until it shines
That you may feel
What I must know
By standing here.
My sons, I bring
These beings home
Into your room.
They are. I am.

Alan Dugan

Elegy

I know but will not tell
you, Aunt Irene, why there

are soapsuds in the whiskey:
Uncle Robert had to have
a drink while shaving. May
there be no bloodshed in your house
this morning of my father's death
and no unkept appearance
in the living, since he has
to wear the rouge and lipstick
of your ceremony, mother,
for the first and last time:
father, hello and goodbye.

Alan Dugan

Coat of Arms
In memory of E.A. Dugan

My father's Memory Book
was warm before the womb
among gymnasium smells
of resolutions put to dust.
The grand tour of his squint
that stopped for photographs
before each sepia Wonder
found Ithaca and ease
beneath the attic dust.
What a joker, like me:
he came into the womb
where I was, poked around
and spat and left and I
was forced out wet
into the cold air. Someone

slapped me and I wept
to have become a traveling man.
Oh I inherited his book
stamped with a coat of arms
self-made from dreams—
a moon and family beast,
a phrase around a shield
boldly nicked with feats
and warm before the womb—
and wondered, laughing, why,
when heroes have come home
from labors out of time
they loll out fatherhood
in baseball-worship, old
underclothes, odd sales jobs
and bad stories often told,
told often, stories often told,
but in one photograph,
the last before the womb,
the dragon had been stuffed
and shipped off home,
authentically killed, and he
is posed in mail, his head
fixed in a photographer's clamp
and Coney Island smile
graced by the cry: "INHIBIT!"
So I learned to rent arms too,
and go out broke without
escutcheon, with a blank
shield against all critics and
a motto of my own
devising on the rim:

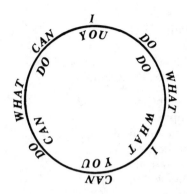

and throw down a left-handed glove
under the cry: "ETCETERA!"

Anthony Hecht

Adam

Hath the rain a father? or who hath begotten the drops of dew?

"Adam, my child, my son,
These very words you hear
Compose the fish and starlight
Of your untroubled dream.
When you awake, my child,
It shall all come true.
Know that it was for you
That all things were begun."

Adam, my child, my son,
Thus spoke Our Father in heaven
To his first, fabled child,

The father of us all.
And I, your father, tell
The words over again
As innumerable men
From ancient times have done.

Tell them again in pain,
And to the empty air.
Where you are men speak
A different mother tongue.
Will you forget our games,
Our hide-and-seek and song?
Child, it will be long
Before I see you again.

Adam, there will be
Many hard hours,
As an old poem says,
Hours of loneliness.
I cannot ease them for you;
They are our common lot.
During them, like as not,
You will dream of me.

When you are crouched away
In a strange clothes closet
Hiding from one who's "It"
And the dark crowds in,
Do not be afraid—
O, if you can, believe
In a father's love
That you shall know some day.

Think of the summer rain
Or seedpearls of the mist;
Seeing the beaded leaf,
Try to remember me.

From far away
I send my blessing out
To circle the great globe.
It shall reach you yet.

Anthony Hecht

Jason
And from America the golden fleece   Marlowe

The room is full of gold.
Is it a chapel? Is that the genuine buzz
Of cherubim, the wingèd goods?
Is it no more than sun that floods
To pool itself at her uncovered breast?
O lights, o numina, behold
How we are gifted. He who never was,
Is, and her fingers bless him and are blessed.

That blessedness is tossed
In a wild, dodging light. Suddenly clear
And poised in heavenly desire
Prophets and eastern saints take fire
And fuse with gold in windows across the way,
And turn to liquid, and are lost.
And now there deepens over lakes of air
A remembered stillness of the seventh day

Borne in on the soft cruise
And sway of birds. Slowly the ancient seas,
Those black, predestined waters rise
Lisping and calm before my eyes,

And Massachusetts rises out of foam
A state of mind in which by twos
All beasts browse among barns and apple trees
As in their earliest peace, and the dove comes home.

Tonight, my dear, when the moon
Settles the radiant dust of every man,
Powders the bedsheets and the floor
With lightness of those gone before,
Sleep then, and dream the story as foretold:
Dream how a little boy alone
With a wooden sword and the top of a garbage can
Triumphs in gardens full of marigold.

Richard Hugo

Here, but Unable to Answer

in memory, Herbert Hugo

A small dawn, sailor. First light glints
off water and it rays across your face
some ill-defined religion. I see you
always on the bridge alone, vigorous
and handsome. Eight bells. You bellow orders.
Your voice rolls back the wind.
Your eyes light numbers on the compass green.

Had I found you lost, I swear
I would have torn the clouds apart right
beneath the north star long enough
for you to fix position, and we'd have gone
sailing, sailing down our boyhood rivers
out to open sea, you proud of my power
over uncooperative sky. What a team

and never to be. You gone to China. I alone
with two old people and in nightmare earth
becoming drier. No new crop. No growth.

Even in war we lived a war apart.
You who desperately wanted combat
stuck piloting new ships from Pittsburgh
to the gulf. Me and my unwanted self
praying the final bomb run out, praying me alone
home safe, then all the others I forgot.
Forgive the bad nerves I brought home,
these hands still trembling with sky, that deafening
dream exploding me awake. Books will call
that war the last one worth the toll.

Father, now you're buried much too close for me
to a busy highway, I still see you up there
on the bridge, night sky wide open and you naming
wisely every star again, your voice enormous
with the power of moon, of tide. I seldom
sail off course. I swim a silent green.
When I dream, the compass lights stay on.

John Logan

Poem for My Son

1

Well, Paul, when you were nine
I wanted to write
and now you're nearly twelve.
For too long I have shelved

this fact
        in an
                in-
accessible part
                of myself.
And the presence of it there
is like a blush
                of shame or
guilt inside the flesh
of my face. A fall
bloom of bril-
                liant gold about
to wilt
        beneath
obscure,
        heavy breath.
Your breath is sure
as the hearty new born
filling up your bronze horn
in the junior high band,
and your cheeks puff with it.
Your pockets bulge with hands
as you grin in the picture
about to speak
balancing on the side edges of your
                                feet.
I have seen your new
beau-
        tiful
body dive
and dance one and a half times
into the pool.
My mind moves back
to where at nine I sat
in the bus on the big girl's lap.

And more than once
                        forgot my lunch
so the one ahead
                in the fourth grade
(believe
        it
            or not
named Glee!)
would give me sections of her
or-
    ange
not knowing it was all prearranged
inside
        my mysterious head.

        2

When I was young
I lived on a farm Grandfather owned:
I remember in the cold
my small damp tongue
stuck on the hand-
                    le of the pump.
My cousin Clark
and I got the calf to lick
us in the barn,
                but then
his father caught
                    us and caught
us too smok-
ing big
        cigars behind the crib!
I carried cobs
                in buckets for the cook-
stove and cranked the separator hard.
Oh, I did

all my chores with a genial hatred.
Sometimes at night I lay
in waves
            of summer grass
feeling inside my chest
the *arching*
                of the search
                            light *shin-*
ing from the distant town.

        3

When I was ten
                nobody said
what it was the dogs did
to each other, or the bull
(whom we never could
                        go near) and
the cow with the gentle bell.
                            The good
                            nuns told
me (I didn't ask)
that my dick
could only carry waste.
But they were wrong.
My son, you shouldn't have
to wait
        as long
as some to learn to love
and find for yourself
a bright, a sweet, calming wife.
There are some things not all fathers know
but if I could I would tell you how.

4

Oh I remember times I wish
I could forget.
Once when the family took a trip
and stopped
            at a motel
you cried and cried.
We thought that you were ill.
Then at last you said
"Why did
        we have
                to move
to this small house?"
And the vacation time
when you got left behind
in the car while the other kids and I climbed
the mountain side.
When we came back you did not feel
well.
    You fiddled with the wheel.
My mind's eye
                goes blank as yours that day.
And once after the divorce,
confused, you asked in a small voice
(a mild one)
Daddy, do you have any children?
I do, Paul. *You* are one.

John Logan

Coming of Age

Driving the new road to Buck's Lake,
I shout toward the pick-up's back
but find they cannot hear me from the cab where I sit
forward with my fond son David
in his blue turquoise brand new truck.
Young sons Paul, Stephen—and Stephen's girl—ride behind
It's David's birthday and we plan
to celebrate it in the sun.
At the lake we leave the truck and seek a private place.
After long experience I am afraid to burn,
so I don't undress as my three kids strip to their trunks,
and fresh, nubile Clara hikes up sharp her bathing strap.
Suddenly David dives, streaks from a high, jutting rock:
a wild swan just turned twenty-one.
I flush and feel alive as he.
Paul, my youngest one, after fast-swimming a full lap,
lies asleep, and the hairs on his legs and belly sweep
as he dries and dreams in the late
summer wind. "Whew," the others shriek
climbing up out of the cold lake.
They shiver underneath the white
fir and sugar pine while they sip
frothing cans of bright colored pop
and beer: there's only one kind of brew they'll drink, since
in all the little towns about,
big David is distributor.
We chat a bit and then they swim clean across the lake!
Their voices flutter like my shadow in the water.
Clara, who could be my daughter,
has the highest voice. I answer,

"Please stay over there a while! I've not finished my thought
But they head home, and I leave my

reveries in the breeze-blown foam,
which wafts to the manzanita and the golden oak.
Their new lives shape in this, my wake.

For David Logan
—1980

Louis Simpson

My Father in the Night Commanding No

My father in the night commanding No
Has work to do. Smoke issues from his lips;
    He reads in silence.
The frogs are croaking and the streetlamps glow.

And then my mother winds the gramophone;
The Bride of Lammermoor begins to shriek—
    Or reads a story
About a prince, a castle, and a dragon.

The moon is glittering above the hill.
I stand before the gateposts of the King—
    So runs the story—
Of Thule, at midnight when the mice are still.

And I have been in Thule! It has come true—
The journey and the danger of the world,
    All that there is
To bear and to enjoy, endure and do.

Landscapes, seascapes...where have I been led?
The names of cities—Paris, Venice, Rome—

Held out their arms.
A feathered god, seductive, went ahead.

Here is my house. Under a red rose tree
A child is swinging, another gravely plays.
    They are not surprised
That I am here; they were expecting me.

And yet my father sits and reads in silence,
My mother sheds a tear, the moon is still,
    And the dark wind
Is murmuring that nothing ever happens.

Beyond his jurisdiction as I move
Do I not prove him wrong? And yet, it's true
    They will not change
There, on the stage of terror and of love.

The actors in that playhouse always sit
In fixed positions—father, mother, child
    With painted eyes.
How sad it is to be a little puppet!

Their heads are wooden. And you once pretended
To understand them! Shake them as you will,
    They cannot speak.
Do what you will, the comedy is ended.

Father, why did you work? Why did you weep,
Mother? Was the story so important?
    "Listen!" the wind
Said to the children, and they fell asleep.

Louis Simpson

Working Late

A light is on in my father's study.
"Still up?" he says, and we are silent,
looking at the harbor lights,
listening to the surf
and the creak of coconut boughs.

He is working late on cases.
No impassioned speech! He argues from evidence,
actually pacing out and measuring,
while the fans revolving on the ceiling
winnow the true from the false.

Once he passed a brass curtain rod
through a head made out of plaster
and showed the jury the angle of fire—
where the murderer must have stood.
For years, all through my childhood,
if I opened a closet...bang!
There would be the dead man's head
with a black hole in the forehead.

All the arguing in the world
will not stay the moon.
She has come all the way from Russia
to gaze for a while in a mango tree
and light the wall of a veranda,
before resuming her interrupted journey
beyond the harbor and the lighthouse
at Port Royal, turning away
from land to the open sea.

Yet, nothing in nature changes, from that
        day to this,
she is still the mother of us all.
I can see the drifting offshore lights,
black posts where the pelicans brood.

And the light that used to shine
at night in my father's study
now shines as late in mine.

Philip Whalen

For My Father

Being a modest man, you wanted
Expected an ordinary child
And here's this large, inscrutable object

ME

(Buddha's mother only dreamed
of a white elephant;
my mother...)

Cross between a TV camera and a rotary press
Busy turning itself into many printed pages
Heavy, a dust-collector, almost impossible
to get off your hands, out of the house
Whatever it was, not an actual child

You recognize parts of the works, ones you first donated
But what are they doing—the flywheel horizontal
Spinning two directions at once
A walking-beam connected to a gear train turning camshafts
Which produces material like this
Sometimes worth money to folks in New York
Or not, nobody knows why.

3:i:58

Edward Field

Visiting Home
(Part IV)

Yiskidor, when he dies I won't know the Hebrew words to say.
Yiskidor, I won't be able to help the soul he doesn't believe
in find rest.
Yiskidor, I go through life cut off from my ancestors.
Yiskidor, I live a life of shit.
Yiskidor, I'm a bum, I'm no man, I'm not even at the
beginning.
Yiskidor, I don't know the prayers.
Yiskidor, I don't know the sacred rites.
Yiskidor, I buried my friend Alfred and it was done badly,
nobody wailed, nobody tore their clothes—
I didn't know you were supposed to,
though somehow I felt like doing it.
Yiskidor, I took a clod of earth from the grave
and have placed it in my shrine with his books
and the letter from Jerusalem telling how he died
of alcohol and drugs like a movie star,
his dogs barking to alert the neighbors.
He always reminded me of Marilyn Monroe—
he had that ultimate glamour
and went around in a cloud of admiration,
though he never felt loved.
Like a good Jew, he went to Jerusalem to die
but his family brought him back
and buried him in Staten Island.
Yiskidor, when the clods hit the coffin I bawled
and everybody turned and stared at me.

Yiskidor, I pray for my mother every way I can
though I don't know the prayers to protect her.
Yiskidor, how she suffers, my mommeh.
I promised I would take her to California when I
grew up

115

and we'd live in a house overlooking the ocean,
just so she wouldn't suffer anymore.
Yiskidor, what is my sacred duty to my parents
but to honor them, both in life and in death,
for they produced me by the holy process,
Yiskidor, and if they fucked me up
they did not know what they were doing.

Yiskidor, and look what they gave me, the gifts,
my life's full of gifts, all my loves.
Yiskidor, for that little boy who didn't know it but was lucky,
with parents that made life hard,
Yiskidor, who complicated things for me
so I could never take the easy path
but had to choose my own
when all I wanted was to be standard:
straight hair, straight nose, straight.
Yiskidor, for that desperate wish I went to sleep with
every night,
"When I wake up I'll look right, be popular,
They'll like me."

Yiskidor, I woke up at last and they liked me
(even if I don't like myself)
so I don't read the "How To Be Popular" books
any more.
Now I read the "How To Be Saved" books.
They all say, Awaken,
follow the path of the heart
which leads to the east.
There is no one to blame any more
and what you become is up to you.

Yiskidor, and I believe them, I can't help it.
My family screams at me, Be skeptical.
I'd like to be but I can't.
Yiskidor, I see I had the perfect parents

for everything has turned out right
like a miracle.

Yiskidor, I had the illusion I could invent my Self,
I thought I could live by the rules of psychiatrists,
Yiskidor, I had the illusion I could get free of history,
not only our history, but my own history.
Yiskidor, but now I must go back to the beginning
if I can find it. It is surely somewhere
inside myself, still trapped
in that defeat at the first breath
when I understood my predicament—
which I chose.

Yiskidor, they have my love, the dear ones who are old now.
Yiskidor, all men and women are my brothers and sisters
now.
Yiskidor, how I love men, now that I have dared
to look in their eyes
and stand my ground as the energies connect.
Yiskidor, if men would reach out and hold each other
they would know we are all brothers.
Yiskidor, I am my father's son, God help me.
Yiskidor, I am my father's son, the heir
to the mess he couldn't solve.
Yiskidor, thank God I am my mother's son too
for what she gave me
is what I survived by.
I cry Mamma, and am healed.
Yiskidor, I am my father's son.
Even if I can't stand it, still
I am.

Harvey Shapiro

Saul's Progress

1.

I told my son:
"Stop trying to screw the monkey's tail
Into his bellybutton.
Originality
Is never its own
Justification.
Some innovations
Get nowhere."

"The Sunday monkeys are my friends,"
He said.
I was on my way down
From the heavenly city
Of the 18th Century philosophers.
He was on his way up,
Almost three.

2.

"Moby Dick is smarter than
The other dicks."
A song to make the
Bad guys happy.
You sang it all day Saturday
With snot-filled nose
And clouded eye,
To raise me
To a fury.

3.

You sit on the crest of a dune
Facing the sea,

Which is beyond sight.
Your anger at me
Makes you play by yourself,
Tell stories to yourself,
Fling out your hurt
To the wide sky's healing.
A red boat in one hand,
A blue in the other,
You begin singing songs
About the weather.
Cliff swallow, brilliant skimmer.

4.

As if he were me, he comes bounding in,
All happiness. I owe him
All happiness. For these years at least.
When he smiles and says, a good time,
I have no notion who else
He has made happy with my happiness.

Donald Justice

Sonnet To My Father

Father, since always now the death to come
Looks naked out from your eyes into mine,
Almost it seems the death to come is mine
And that I also shall be overcome,
Father, and call for breath when you succumb,
And struggle for your hand as you for mine
In hope of comfort that shall not be mine

Till for this last of me the angel come.
But, father, though with you in part I die
And glimpse beforehand that eternal place
Where we forget the pain that brought us there,
Father, and though you go before me there,
And leave this likeness only in your place,
Yet while I live, you do not wholly die.

Donald Justice

Sonatina in Yellow

Du schnell vergehendes Daguerreotyp
in meinen langsamer vergehenden Händen.—Rilke

The pages of the album,
As they are turned, turn yellow; a word,
Once spoken, obsolete,
No longer what was meant. Say it.
The meanings come, or come back later,
Unobtrusive, taking their places.

Think of the past. Think of forgetting the past.
It was an exercise requiring further practice;
A difficult exercise, played through by someone else.
Overheard from another room, now,
It seems full of mistakes.
                              So the voice of your father,
Rising as from the next room still
With all the remote but true affection of the dead,
Repeats itself, insists,
Insisting you must listen, rises
In the familiar pattern of reproof

For some childish error, a nap disturbed,
Or vase, broken or overturned;
Rises and subsides. And you do listen.
Listen and forget. Practice forgetting.

Forgotten sunlight still
Blinds the eyes of faces in the album.
The faces fade, and there is only
A sort of meaning that comes back,
Or for the first time comes, but comes too late
To take the places of the faces.

                    Remember
The dead air of summer. Remember
The trees drawn up to their full height like fathers,
The underworld of shade you entered at their feet.
Enter the next room. Enter it quietly now,
Not to disturb your father sleeping there. *He stirs.*
Notice his clothes, how scrupulously clean,
Unwrinkled from the nap; his face, freckled with work,
Smoothed by a passing dream. The vase
Is not yet broken, the still young roses
Drink there from perpetual waters. *He rises, speaks . . .*

Repeat it now, no one was listening.
So your hand moves, moving across the keys,
And slowly the keys grow darker to the touch.

Donald Justice

Men at Forty

Men at forty
Learn to close softly

The doors to rooms they will not be
Coming back to.

At rest on a stair landing,
They feel it moving
Beneath them now like the deck of a ship,
Though the swell is gentle.

And deep in mirrors
They rediscover
The face of the boy as he practices tying
His father's tie there in secret

And the face of that father,
Still warm with the mystery of lather.
They are more fathers than sons themselves now.
Something is filling them, something

That is like the twilight sound
Of the crickets, immense,
Filling the woods at the foot of the slope
Behind their mortgaged houses.

Stanley Moss

Fishermen

My father made a synagogue of a boat.
I fish in ghettos, cast toward the lilypads,
strike rock and roil the unworried waters;
I in my father's image: rusty and off hinge,
the fishing box between us like a covenant.
I reel in, the old lure bangs against the boat.

As the sun shines I take his word for everything.
My father snarls his line, spends half an hour
unsnarling mine. Eel, sunfish and bullhead
are not for me. At seven I cut my name for bait.
The worm gnawed toward the mouth of my name.
"Why are the words for temple and school
the same," I asked, "And why a school of fish?"
My father does not answer. On a bad cast
my fish strikes, breaks water, takes the line.

Into a world of good and evil, I reel
a creature languished in the flood. I tear out
the lure, hooks cold. I catch myself,
two hooks through the hand,
blood on the floor of the synagogue. The wound
is purple, shows a mouth of white birds;
hook and gut dangle like a rosary,
another religion in my hand.
I'm ashamed of this image of crucifixion.
A Jew's image is a reading man.
My father tears out the hooks, returns to his book,
a nineteenth-century history of France.
Our war is over:
death hooks the corner of his lips.
The wrong angel takes over the lesson.

Stanley Moss

The Branch

Since they were morose in August,
not worth saving,

I paid to have the junipers torn out
trunk and root, the roots had enough strength
to pull the truck back down so hard
the wheels broke the brick walk.

Heaped in front of my house,
cousins of the tree of mercy,
the green and dry gray branches
that did not suffer
but had beauty to lose.
Damp roots, what do I know
of the tenderness of earth,
the girlish blond dust?
Rather than have the branches dumped or burned
I dragged them to the bulkhead
and pushed them into the sea.

I know the story of a tree:
of Adam's skull at the foot of Jesus crucified,
of the cross made of timbers nailed together
that Roman soldiers saved from the destroyed temple,
that King Solomon built from a great tree
that rooted and flourished
from a branch of the tree of mercy
planted in dead Adam's mouth,
that the branch was given
to Adam's third son Seth by an angel
that stopped him outside the wall
when he returned to the garden,
that the angel warned him
that he could not save his father
who was old and ill
with oils or tears or prayers.

Go in darkness, mouth to mouth
is the command.
I kiss the book,
not wanting to speak

of the suffering I have caused.
Sacred and defiled,
my soul is right
to deal with me in secret.

Stanley Moss

Centaur Song

A creature half horse, half human,
my father herded his mares and women together
for song, smell, and conversation. He taught me
to love wine, music, and English poetry.
Like the Greeks he left the temple's interior
for priests, he observed outside
where he could see the pediment and caryatids.
If he saw a beauty out walking, or on a journey,
the proper centaur offered to carry her
over ice, or across a river,—he'd bolt
to the edge of a wood, a place of sunlight,
the light itself stunned and entertained.
He slid her gently down his back,
held her to him with one hand and a hoof.
His hoofs cut, how could he touch with tenderness?
I feel his loneliness when I am just with horses
or just with humans. For a time
he had himself tied to a tree,
so he could not go to either one.
Now his city crushed deep in the ground
has disappeared in darkness,
—which is a theme for music.
He licked the blood from a trembling foal,
he galloped back to his books.

125

Stanley Moss

In Front of a Poster of Garibaldi

1

When my Italian son
admired a poster of Garibaldi
in the piazzetta of Venice,
a national father in a red shirt,
gold chain, Moroccan fez and fancy beard,
I wished the boy knew the Lincoln
who read after a day's work,
the honesty, the commoner.
My knees hurt from my life and playing soccer
—not that I see Lincoln splashing with his kids
in the Potomac. Lord knows where his dead son led him.

2

My son tells me *Fortuna* could have put
Lincoln and Garibaldi in Venice—
Garibaldi in red silk, Lincoln
in a stovepipe hat black as a gondola.
My son mimics Garibaldi:
"Lincoln you may be the only man in the piazza
to log down the Mississippi
and walk back the 1500 miles to Illinois
but you are still a man who calls all pasta macaroni.
How do you know where you are going?
Your shoes are straights, no lasts,
no right or left, no fashion, white socks.
How can the President of the United States
make such a *brutta figura?*"

3

I can't speak for Lincoln,
anymore than I can sing for Caruso,

—toward the end when Caruso sang
his mouth filled with blood.
Not every poet bites into his own jugular,
some hunger, some observe the intelligence of clouds.
I was surprised to see a heart come out
of the torn throat of a snake. I know a poet
whose father blew his brains out
before his son was born, still leads his son
into the unknown, the unknowable.

4

My son tells me I must not forget
Garibaldi fought for liberty in six countries
including Uruguay, he refused the command
of a corps that Lincoln offered,
asked to be head of the Union armies
and an immediate declaration against slavery,
he was the King's flag, defeated
the papal armies in 1866,
which gave the Jews equality in Italy,
looking to the North, he supported the Danes against
the Swedes, fought against the Austrians all his life,
fought with the French, who had been his enemy
against the Prussians—he'd shoot a trooper
for stealing a chicken.

5

I've always had a preference
for politics you could sing
on the stage of the Scala.
I give my son Lincoln and Garibaldi
as guardian angels.
May he join a party and a temple
that offer a chair to the starving and unrespectable.
We come from stock that on the day of atonement

ask forgiveness for theft, murder, lies, betrayal,
for all the sins and crimes of the congregation.
May he take his girls and bride to Venice,
may the blessings come like pigeons.
Lincoln waves from his gondola and whispers,
"I don't know what the soul is
but whatever it is, I know it can humble itself."

Gerald Stern

The Sensitive Knife

Every day the dark blue sky of brother Van Gogh
gets closer and closer,
and every day the blue gentians of brother Lawrence
darken my eyes.
It is blue wherever I go,
walking the towpath,
climbing the stone island,
swimming the river,
and everywhere I sit or kneel
the blue goes through me like a sensitive knife.

I am following my own conception now
and during the night I flap my two-foot wings
in the black locusts.
I move thoughtfully from branch to branch,
always loving the stiffness and shyness
of the old giants.
I think of my own legs as breaking off
or my wings coming loose in the wind
or my blossoms dropping onto the ground.

Across the river the sticks are coming to life
and Mithras and Moses and Jesus are swaying and bowing
in all directions.
I swim carefully through the blood
and land on my feet on the side of Carpenter's Hill.
There on a flat rock
my father is placing the shank bone
and the roasted egg on a white napkin.
I climb over the rhododendrons and the dead trees to meet him.

Gerald Stern

The Dancing

In all these rotten shops, in all this broken furniture
and wrinkled ties and baseball trophies and coffee pots
I have never seen a post-War Philco
with the automatic eye
nor heard Ravel's *Bolero* the way I did
in 1945 in that tiny living room
on Beechwood Boulevard, nor danced as I did
then, my knives all flashing, my hair all streaming,
my mother red with laughter, my father cupping
his left hand under his armpit, doing the dance
of old Ukraine, the sound of his skin half drum,
half fart, the world at last a meadow,
the three of us whirling and singing, the three of us
screaming and falling, as if we were dying,
as if we could never stop—in 1945—
in Pittsburgh, beautiful filthy Pittsburgh, home
of the evil Mellons, 5,000 miles away
from the other dancing—in Poland and Germany—
oh God of mercy, oh wild God.

A.R. Ammons

My Father Used to Tell of an

My father used to tell of an
old lady so old
they ran her down and knocked
her in the head with
a lightered knot
to bury her (then
there was another
one so old
she dried up and turned
to something good to eat)

what my father enjoyed
most—in terms of pure,
high pleasure—was
scaring things: I remember
one day he and
I were coming up in Aunt
Lottie's yard
when there were these
ducks ambling
along in the morning sun,
a few drakes, hens, and a string of
ducklings,
and my father took off his
strawhat and
shot it spinning out sailing in
a fast curving glide over the
ducks so they
thought they were being
swooped by a hawk,
and they just, it looked
like, hunkered down on their
rearends and slid all the
way like they were

greased right under the house
  (in those days houses
  were built up off the ground)
my father laughed the purest,
highest laughter
till he bent over
thinking about those
ducks sliding under
there over nothing

my father, if you could rise
up to where he was at, knew
how to get fun straight
out of things
  he was a legend
  in my lifetime

I remember when he was so
strong he could carry me and
my sister, one leaning to
each shoulder, with our
feet in the big wooden slop bucket:
he died with not a leg
to stand on

Robert Bly

For My Son, Noah, Ten Years Old

Night and day arrive, and day after day goes by,
and what is old remains old, and what is young remains young, and
    grows old,

and the lumber pile does not grow younger, nor the weathered
    by fours lose their darkness,
but the old tree goes on, the barn stands without help so ma
    years,
the advocate of darkness and night is not lost.

The horse swings around on one leg, steps, and turns,
the chicken flapping claws onto the roost, its wings whelpin
    whalloping,
but what is primitive is not to be shot out into the night and
    the dark.
And slowly the kind man comes closer, loses his rage, sits do
    at table.

So I am proud only of those days that we pass in undivided
    tenderness,
when you sit drawing, or making books, stapled, with messages
    the world . . .
or coloring a man with fire coming out of his hair.
Or we sit at a table, with small tea carefully poured;
so we pass our time together, calm and delighted.

Robert Bly

Finding the Father

   This body offers to carry us for nothing—as the ocean
carries logs—so on some days the body wails with its great
energy, it smashes up the boulders, lifting small crabs, that
flow around the sides. Someone knocks on the door, we do
not have time to dress. He wants us to come with him

through the blowing and rainy streets, to the dark house.
We will go there, the body says, and there find the father
whom we have never met, who wandered in a snowstorm
the night we were born, who then lost his memory, and has
lived since longing for his child, whom he saw only
once . . . while he worked as a shoemaker, as a cattle herder
in Australia, as a restaurant cook who painted at night.
When you light the lamp you will see him. He sits there
behind the door . . . the eyebrows so heavy, the forehead so
light . . . lonely in his whole body, waiting for you.

Robert Bly

My Father's Wedding
1924

Today, lonely for my father, I saw
a log, or branch,
long, bent, ragged, bark gone.
I felt lonely for my father when I saw it.
It was the log
that lay near my uncle's old milk wagon.

Some men live with an invisible limp,
stagger, or drag
a leg. Their sons are often angry.
Only recently I thought:
Doing what you want . . .
Is that like limping? Tracks of it show in sand.

Have you seen those giant bird-
men of Bhutan?

Men in bird masks, with pig noses, dancing,
teeth like a dog's, sometimes
dancing on one bad leg!
They do what they want, the dog's teeth say that!

But I grew up without dogs' teeth,
showed a whole body,
left only clear tracks in sand.
I learned to walk swiftly, easily,
no trace of a limp.
I even leaped a little. Guess where my defect is!

Then what? If a man, cautious
hides his limp,
Somebody has to limp it! Things
do it; the surroundings limp.
House walls get scars,
the car breaks down; matter, in drudgery, takes it up.

On my father's wedding day,
no one was there
to hold him. Noble loneliness
held him. Since he never asked for pity
his friends thought he
was whole. Walking alone, he could carry it.

He came in limping. It was a simple
wedding, three
or four people. The man in black,
lifting the book, called for order.
And the invisible bride
stepped forward, before his own bride.

He married the invisible bride, not his own.
In her left
breast she carried the three drops
that wound and kill. He already had

his barklike skin then,
made rough especially to repel the sympathy

he longed for, didn't need, and wouldn't accept.
They stopped. So
the words are read. The man in black
speaks the sentence. When the service
is over, I hold him
in my arms for the first time and the last.

After that he was alone
and I was alone.
No friends came; he invited none.
His two-story house he turned
into a forest,
where both he and I are the hunters.

Robert Creeley

A Variation

1

My son who is stranger
than he should be, outgrown
at five, the normal—

luck is against him!
Unfit for the upbringing he would otherwise
have got, I have no hopes for him.

I leave him alone.

I leave him to his own
devices, having pity not so much that he is
strange

but that I am him.

2

Myself, who am stranger
than I should be, outgrown
at two, the normal—

luck is against me. Unfit
for the upbringing I would otherwise
have got, I have no hopes.

I leave him alone.

I leave him to his own
devices, having pity not so much for
myself, for why should that happen

but that he is me, as much as I am him.

Allen Ginsberg

Don't Grow Old

I

Old Poet, Poetry's final subject glimmers months ahead
Tender mornings, Paterson roofs snowcovered
Vast
Sky over City Hall tower, Eastside Park's grass terraces &
    tennis courts beside Passaic River

Parts of ourselves gone, sister Rose's apartments, brown
    corridor'd high schools—
Too tired to go out for a walk, too tired to end the War
Too tired to save body
too tired to be heroic
The real close at hand as the stomach
liver pancreas rib
Coughing up gastric saliva
Marriages vanished in a cough
Hard to get up from the easy chair
Hands white   feet speckled   a blue toe   stomach big
    breasts hanging thin
hair white on the chest
too tired to take off shoes and black sox

Jan 12, 1976

II

He'll see no more Times Square
honkytonk movie marquees, bus stations at midnight
Nor the orange sun ball
rising thru treetops east toward New York's skyline
His velvet armchair facing the window will be empty
He won't see the moon over house roofs
or sky over Paterson's streets.

Feb 26, 1976

III

Wasted arms, feeble knees
    80 years old, hair thin and white
        cheek bonier than I'd remembered—
head bowed on his neck, eyes opened
    now and then, he listened—

I read my father Wordsworth's *Intimations of Immortality*
"...*trailing clouds of glory do we come*
from God, who is our home..."
"That's beautiful," he said, "but it's not true."

"When I was a boy, we had a house
    on Boyd Street, Newark—the backyard
        was a big empty lot full of bushes and tall grass,
    I always wondered what was behind those trees,
When I grew older, I walked around the block,
    and found out what was back there—
        it was a glue factory."

May 18, 1976

IV

Will that happen to me?
Of course, it'll happen to thee.

Will my arms whither away?
Yes yr arm hair will turn grey.

Will my knees grow weak & collapse?
Your knees will need crutches perhaps.

Will my chest get thin?
Your breasts will be hanging skin.

Where will go—my teeth?
You'll keep the ones beneath.

What'll happen to my bones?
They'll get mixed up with the stones.

June 1976

FATHER DEATH BLUES

Hey Father Death, I'm flying home
Hey poor man, you're all alone
Hey old daddy, I know where I'm going

Father Death, Don't cry any more
Mama's there, underneath the floor
Brother Death, please mind the store

Old Aunty Death   Don't hide your bones
Old Uncle Death   I hear your groans
O Sister Death   how sweet your moans

O Children Deaths go breathe your breaths
Sobbing breasts'll ease your Deaths
Pain is gone, tears take the rest

Genius Death   your art is done
Lover Death your body's gone
Father Death   I'm coming home

Guru Death your words are true
Teacher Death I do thank you
For inspiring me to sing this Blues

Buddha Death, I wake with you
Dharma Death, your mind is new
Sangha Death, we'll work it through

Suffering is what was born
Ignorance made me forlorn
Tearful truths I cannot scorn

Father Breath once more farewell

Birth you gave was no thing ill
My heart is still, as time will tell.

July 8, 1976 (over Lake Michigan)

VI

Near the Scrap Yard my Father'll be Buried
Near Newark Airport my father'll be
Under a Winston Cigarette sign buried
On Exit 14 Turnpike NJ South
Through the tollgate Service Road 1 my father buried
Past Merchants Refrigerating concrete on the cattailed mars
past the Budweiser Anheuser-Busch brick brewery
in B'Nai Israel Cemetery behind a green painted iron fence
where there used to be a paint factory and farms
where Pennick makes chemicals now
under the Penn Central power Station
transformers & wires, at the borderline
between Elizabeth and Newark, next to Aunt Rose
Gaidemack, near Uncle Harry Meltzer
one grave over from Abe's wife Anna my father'll be buried.

9 July 1976

VII

What's to be done about Death?
Nothing, nothing
Stop going to school No. 6 Paterson, N.J., in 1937?
Freeze time tonight, with a headache, at quarter to 2 A.M.?
Not go to Father's funeral tomorrow morn?
Not go back to Naropa   teach Buddhist poetics all summ
Not be buried in the cemetery near Newark Airport some c

July 11, 1976

140

VIII

Twenty-eight years before on the living room couch he'd
     stared at me, I said
"I want to see a psychiatrist—I have sexual difficulties—
     homosexuality"
I'd come home from troubled years as a student. This was
     the weekend I would talk with him.
A look startled his face, "You mean you like to take men's
     penises in your mouth?"
Equally startled, "No, no," I lied, "that isn't what it means."

Now he lay naked in the bath, hot water draining beneath
     his shanks.
Strong shouldered Peter, once ambulance attendant, raised
     him up
in the tiled room. We toweled him dry, arms under his,
     bathrobe over his shoulder—
he tottered thru the door to his carpeted bedroom
sat on the soft mattress edge, exhausted, and coughed up
     watery phlegm.
We lifted his swollen feet talcum'd white, put them thru
     pyjama legs,
tied the cord round his waist, and held the nightshirt sleeve
     open for his hand, slow.
Mouth drawn in, his false teeth in a dish, he turned his head
     round,
looking up at Peter to smile ruefully, "Don't ever grow old."

IX

At my urging, my eldest nephew came
to keep his grandfather company, maybe sleep overnight in
     the apartment.
He had no job, and was homeless anyway.
All afternoon he read the papers and looked at old movies.

141

Later dusk, television silent, we sat on a soft-pillowed couch,
Louis sat in his easy-chair that swivelled and could lean back
"So what kind of job are you looking for?"
"Dishwashing, but someone told me it makes your hands'
　　skin scaly red."
"And what about officeboy?" His grandson finished high-
　　school with marks too poor for college.
"It's unhealthy inside airconditioned buildings under fluor-
　　escent light."
The dying man looked at him, nodding at the specimen.
He began his advice. "You might be a taxidriver, but what if
　　a car crashed into you? They say you can get mugged
　　too.
"Or you could get a job as a sailor, but the ship could sink,
　　you could get drowned.
"Maybe you should try a career in the grocery business, but
　　a box of bananas could slip from the shelf,
"you could hurt your head. Or if you were a waiter, you
　　could slip and fall down with a loaded tray, & have to
　　pay for the broken glasses.
"Maybe you should be a carpenter, but your thumb might
　　get hit by a hammer.
"Or a lifeguard—but the undertow at Belmar beach is dan-
　　gerous, and you could catch a cold.
"Or a doctor, but sometimes you could cut your hand with a
　　scalpel that had germs, you could get sick & die."

Later, in bed after twilight, glasses off, he said to his wife
"Why doesn't he comb his hair? It falls all over his eyes, how
　　can he see?
Tell him to go home soon, I'm too tired."

October 5, 1978

X
Resigned

A year before visiting a handsome poet and my Tibetan guru,
      Guests after supper on the mountainside
we admired the lights of Boulder spread glittering below
        through a giant glass window—
After coffee, my father bantered wearily
"Is life worth living? Depends on the liver—"
The Lama smiled to his secretary—
It was an old pun I'd heard in childhood.
Then he fell silent, looking at the floor
      and sighed, head bent heavy
        talking to no one—
           "What can you do...?"

October 6, 1978

James Merrill

Scenes of Childhood
for Claude Fredericks

My mother's lamp once out,
I press a different switch:
A field within the dim
White screen ignites,
Vibrating to the rapt
Mechanical racket
Of a real noon field's
Crickets and gnats.

And to its candid heart
I move with heart ajar,
With eyes that smart less
From pollen or heat
Than from the buried day
Now rising like a moon,
Shining, unwinding
Its taut white sheet.

Two or three bugs that lit
Earlier upon the blank
Sheen, all peaceable
Insensibility, drowse
As she and I cannot
Under the risen flood
Of thirty years ago—
A tree, a house

We had then, a late sun,
A door from which the primal
Figures jerky and blurred
As lightning bugs
From lanterns issue, next
To be taken for stars,
For fates. With knowing smiles
And beaded shrugs

My mother and two aunts
Loom on the screen. Their plucked
Brows pucker, their arms encircle
One another.
Their ashen lips move.
From the love seat's gloom
A quiet chuckle escapes
My white-haired mother

To see in that final light
A man's shadow mount
Her dress. And now she is
Advancing, sister-
less, but followed by
A fair child, or fury—
Myself at four, in tears.
I raise my fist,

Strike, she kneels down. The man's
Shadow afflicts us both.
Her voice behind me says
It might go slower.
I work dials, the film jams.
Our headstrong old projector
Glares at the scene which promptly
Catches fire.

Puzzled, we watch ourselves
Turn red and black, gone up
In a puff of smoke now coiling
Down fierce beams.
I switch them off. A silence.
Your father, she remarks,
Took those pictures; later
Says pleasant dreams,

Rises and goes. Alone
I gradually fade and cool.
Night scatters me with green
Rustlings, thin cries.
Out there between the pines
Have begun shining deeds,
Some low, inconstant (these
Would be fireflies),

Others as in high wind
Aflicker, staying lit.

There are nights we seem to ride
With cross and crown
Forth under them, through fumes,
Coils, the whole rattling epic—
Only to leap clear-eyed
From eiderdown,

Asleep to what we'd seen.
Father already fading—
Who focused your life long
Through little frames,
Whose microscope, now deep
In purple velvet, first
Showed me the skulls of flies,
The fur, the flames

Etching the jaws—father:
Shrunken to our true size.
Each morning, back of us,
Fields wail and shimmer.
To go out is to fall
Under fresh spells, cool web
And stinging song new-hatched
Each day, all summer.

A minute galaxy
About my head will easily
Needle me back. The day's
Inaugural *Damn*
Spoken, I start to run,
Inane, like them, but breathing
In and out the sun
And air I am.

The son and heir! In the dark
It makes me catch my breath
And hear, from upstairs, hers—
That faintest hiss

And slither, as of life
Escaping into space,
Having led its characters
To the abyss

Of night. Immensely still
The heavens glisten. One broad
Path of vague stars is floating
Off, a shed skin
Of all whose fine cold eyes
First told us, locked in ours:
You are the heroes without name
Or origin.

Frank O'Hara

To My Dead Father

Don't call to me father
wherever you are I'm
still your little son
running through the dark

I couldn't do what you
say even if I could hear
your roses no longer grow
my heart's black as their

bed their dainty thorns
have become my face's
troublesome stubble you
must not think of flowers

And do not frighten my
blue eyes with hazel flecks
or thicken my lips when
I face my mirror don't ask

that I be other than your
strange son understanding
minor miracles not death
father I am alive! father

forgive the roses and me

W.D. Snodgrass

Setting Out

Staying here, we turn inflexible,
Stiffening under laws that drive
Sap through the tight stems,
Roots to break down rock;
Relentless as the fall
Of rhymes in a folk ballad.
You are called toward someone free
To come or go as the wind's whim,
Casual as the air whistles,
Trembling all that stands with
Mortal touch, while your hand
Slips through every which way.

Here, we find ourselves unstable
As our fields: crops, cloud-
shadows wash across us;

The various weed-flowers fade
To flat snow; dogs tear
Our deer; streams flow again...
You are drawn to someone constant
As a room where the costly wallpaper
Blooms in half-light,
Where at last somebody dearly
Loved is always almost
Ready to appear.

We know we turn exacting,
Monotonous as the hours
Wheel, as the seasons
Wheel, as the arrogant
Stars turn wheeling on their
Cold, determined track.
Go, then, find someone tender
As a child's eyelid closing
In his first sleep, shy
As the warm scent we all seek,
That mild and absent voice
Numbing the sense away.

Perhaps, who knows, in so much
Searching you may not be lost;
Paths you take may take you
Into comfort past our thought;
It may be the finding
Won't enervate your grasp.
You can find us here, still
Going about our rounds,
Fingering out the beat
Of old songs, fixed on ways
Worn out as a star chart,
Unimaginably far.

John Ashbery

A Boy

I'll do what the raids suggest,
Dad, and that other livid window,
But the tide pushes an awful lot of monsters
And I think it's my true fate.

It had been raining but
It had not been raining.

No one could begin to mop up this particular mess.
Thunder lay down in the heart.
"My child, I love any vast electrical disturbance."
Disturbance! Could the old man, face in the rainweed,

Ask more smuttily? By night it charged over plains,
Driven from Dallas and Oregon, always *whither,*
Why not now? The boy seemed to have fallen
From shelf to shelf of someone's rage.

That night it rained on the boxcars, explaining
The thought of the pensive cabbage roses near the boxcars.
My boy. Isn't there something I asked you once?
What happened? It's also farther to the corner
Aboard the maple furniture. *He*
Couldn't lie. He'd tell 'em by their syntax.

But listen now in the flood.
They're throwing up behind the lines.
Dry fields of lightning rise to receive
The observer, the mincing flag. *An unendurable age.*

Paul Carroll

Father

How sick I get
of your ghost. And
of looking at this tintype on my desk
of you as a cocky kid—
Kilkenny's coast, rocks & suncracked turf
giving the resilience to your countenance
as you try to seem so nonchalant, posing
in a rented Sunday morning-suit
spats & bowler hat:
a greenhorn off the boat. Yet something in

that twist of fist, knuckles taut
around the cane-knob, shows
how you already seem to know you will transform
that old cow-pasture of Hyde Park
into your own oyster.

The way you did.

And that other picture—
stuck somewhere in the dresser drawer
among the Christmas handkerchiefs,
the rubbers, poems & busted rosary beads.
Posed beneath 3 palms
on Tampa Beach's boardwalk,
a stocky man who made his millions by himself.
And can quarrel with congressmen from Washington
about the New Deal bank acts.
Or call Mayor Kelly crooked to his face.

Hair, bone,
          brains & cock & skin
rotten in the earth these 16 years.
     Remember, father, how Monseignor Keelty
     (whose mouth you always said
     looked exactly like a turkey's ass)
boomed out Latin above your coffin at Mt. Olivet?

     But as the raw October rain
     rasped against our limousine
guiding the creeping cars back into Chicago,
          Jack, your first born,
picked his nose:
          and for an instant flicked a look
                    to ask if I too knew
                    you were dead for good—
          St. Patrick's paradise a club
          for priests & politicians
                    you wouldn't get caught dead in.

You used to like to call me 'Bill.' And kiss me.
Or take me to the Brookfield Zoo. Or stuff
     english toffee in my mouth—but always
     only after you had cursed
               & with a bedroom slipper whacked
the tar out of Jack. This morning, father,
          broke as usual,
          no woman in my bed,
     I threw 6 bucks away
     for a shave & haircut at the Drake.
     And looked again for you. On Oak St. beach

gazing beyond the bathers & the boats
I suddenly searched the horizon, father,
for that old snapshot of Picasso
                & his woman Dora Maar.
      Picasso bald & 60. But both
            in exaltation, emerging
    with incredible sexual dignity
            from the waters of the Golfe Juan.

The sun tattooed light on the lake.
      A red bone of a fish.
            The semen of the ghost.

              I left the lake. But tripped
              in the quick dark
of the Division St. underpass. Then picked a way past
           newspaper scraps, puddles
        & a puckered beachball.
    I looked for dirty drawings on the wall.
  Traffic crunches overhead.
This underpass is endless.

W.S. Merwin

The Waving of a Hand

    First rose a low shore   pastures green to the water
that my father must have seen   but did he know it at the time
and maybe it seemed to him then   that he was arriving

a few white facades   far off on the land's edge
lighthouse not yet flashing   small coast guard station
all faintly gleaming   under low sky
by the wide river mouth   late in the day
cold wind sweeping   green estuary
but everything still   calm and as it should be
     water sound sliding   close by under wood
everyone lying down   in the thin vessel
except the one sailor   leaning against the mast
face never seen   turned away forward
catching last sunlight   eyes toward the sea
waves out there suddenly blue   and sky darkening
     yet I was standing   in an old wooden house
where surely my father had stood   but had he known it th
I was among friends   he had never met
     out in back through the window   the same quiet yard
and small wooden study   beyond it under trees
it was growing dark in the room   but no one turned a ligh
and the next time   I looked through that window
there was nothing to see in the yard   but a cloud
a white cloud   full of moonlight
and I tapped someone's shoulder   and we both stared
     then we talked of other things   I did not stay
soon it was really night   I ate with friends it rained
three times I climbed   a long staircase
the first time and the second   someone was at the top
     hundreds of miles   to the west
my father died   just before one in the morning

W.S. Merwin

Yesterday

My friend says I was not a good son
you understand
I say yes I understand

he says I did not go
to see my parents very often you know
and I say yes I know

even when I was living in the same city he says
maybe I would go there once
a month or maybe even less
I say oh yes

he says the last time I went to see my father
I say the last time I saw my father

he says the last time I saw my father
he was asking me about my life
how I was making out and he
went into the next room
to get something to give me

oh I say
feeling again the cold
of my father's hand the last time

he says and my father turned
in the doorway and saw me
look at my wristwatch and he
said you know I would like you to stay
and talk with me

oh yes I say

but if you are busy he said
I don't want you to feel that you
have to
just because I'm here

I say nothing

he says my father
said maybe
you have important work you are doing
or maybe you should be seeing
somebody I don't want to keep you

I look out the window
my friend is older than I am
he says and I told my father it was so
and I got up and left him then
you know

though there was nowhere I had to go
and nothing I had to do

Galway Kinnell

Lastness
(*Part 2*)

A black bear sits alone
in the twilight, nodding from side
to side, turning slowly around and around
on himself, scuffing the four-footed
circle into the earth. He sniffs the sweat
in the breeze, he understands

a creature, a death-creature
watches from the fringe of the trees,
finally he understands
I am no longer here, he himself
from the fringe of the trees watches
a black bear
get up, eat a few flowers, trudge away,
all his fur glistening
in the rain.

And what glistening! Sancho Fergus,
my boychild, had such great shoulders,
when he was born his head
came out, the rest of him stuck. And he opened
his eyes: his head out there all alone
in the room, he squinted with pained,
barely unglued eyes at the ninth-month's
blood splashing beneath him
on the floor. And almost
smiled, I thought, almost forgave it all in advance.

When he came wholly forth
I took him up in my hands and bent
over and smelled
the black, glistening fur
of his head, as empty space
must have bent
over the newborn planet
and smelled the grasslands and the ferns.

Galway Kinnell

Fergus Falling

He climbed to the top
of one of those million white pines
set out across the emptying pastures
of the fifties—some program to enrich the rich
and rebuke the forefathers
who cleared it all once with ox and axe—
climbed to the top, probably to get out
of the shadow
not of those forefathers but of this father,
and saw for the first time,
down in its valley, Bruce Pond, giving off
its little steam in the afternoon,

pond where Clarence Akley came on Sunday mornings to
cut down the cedars around the shore, I'd sometimes
hear the slow spondees of his work, he's gone,
where Milton Norway came up behind me while I was
fishing and stood awhile before I knew he was there, he's
the one who put the cedar shingles on the house, some
have curled or split, a few have blown off, he's gone,
where Gus Newland logged in the cold snap of '58, the only
man willing to go into those woods that never got warmer
than ten below, he's gone,
pond where two wards of the state wandered on Halloween,
the National Guard searched for them in November, in
vain, the next fall a hunter found their skeletons huddled
together, in vain, they're gone,
pond where an old fisherman in a rowboat sits, drowning
hooked worms, when he goes he's replaced and is never
gone,

and when Fergus
saw the pond for the first time
in the clear evening, saw its oldness down there

in its old place in the valley, he became heavier suddenly in his bones,
the way fledglings do just before they fly,
and the soft pine cracked...

I would not have heard his cry
if my electric saw had been working,
its carbide teeth speeding through the bland spruce of our
    time, or burning
black circles into some scavenged hemlock plank,
like dark circles under eyes
when the brain thinks too close to the skin,
but I was sawing by hand and I heard that cry
as though he were attacked; we ran out,
when we bent over him he said, "Galway, Inés, I saw a pond!"
His face went gray, his eyes fluttered closed a frightening
    moment....

Yes, a pond
that lets off its mist
on clear afternoons of August, in that valley
to which many have come, for their reasons,
from which many have gone, a few for their reasons,
    most not,
where even now an old fisherman only the pinetops can see
sits in the dry gray wood of his rowboat, waiting for pickerel.

Galway Kinnell

After Making Love We Hear Footsteps

For I can snore like a bullhorn
or play loud music

or sit up talking with any reasonably sober Irishman
and Fergus will only sink deeper
into his dreamless sleep, which goes by all in one flash,
but let there be that heavy breathing
or a stifled come-cry anywhere in the house
and he will wrench himself awake
and make for it on the run—as now, we lie together,
after making love, quiet, touching along the length of our b
familiar touch of the long-married,
and he appears—in his baseball pajamas, it happens,
the neck opening so small
he has to screw them on, which one day may make him wo
about the mental capacity of baseball players—
and flops down between us and hugs us and snuggles
    himself to sleep,
his face gleaming with satisfaction at being this very child.

In the half darkness we look at each other
and smile
and touch arms across this little, startlingly muscled body—
this one whom habit of memory propels to the ground of his m
sleeper only the mortal sounds can sing awake,
this blessing love gives again into our arms.

James Wright

The Revelation

Stress of his anger set me back
To musing over time and space.
The apple branches dripping black
Divided light across his face.

Towering beneath the broken tree,
he seemed a stony shade to me.
He spoke no language I could hear
For long with my distracted ear.

Between his lips and my delight
In blowing wind, a bird-song rose.
And soon in fierce, blockading light
The planet's shadow hid his face.
And all that strongly molded bone
Of chest and shoulder soon were gone,
Devoured among the solid shade.
Assured his angry voice was dead,

And satisfied his judging eyes
Had given over plaguing me,
I stood to let the darkness rise—
My darkness, gathering in the tree,
The field, the swollen shock of hay,
Bank of the creek half washed away.
Lost in my self, and unaware
Of love, I took the evening air.

I blighted, for a moment's length,
My father out of sight and sound;
Prayed to annihilate his strength,
The proud legs planted on the ground.
Why should I hear his angry cry
Or bear the damning of his eye?
Anger for anger I could give,
And murder for my right to live.

The moon rose. Lucidly the moon
Ran skimming shadows off the trees.
To strip all shadow but its own
Down to the perfect mindlessness.
Yet suddenly the moonlight caught
My father's fingers reaching out,

The strong arm begging me for love,
Loneliness I knew nothing of.

And weeping in the nakedness
Of moonlight and agony,
His blue eyes lost their barrenness
And bore a blossom out to me.
And as I ran to give it back,
The apple branches, dripping black,
Trembled across the lunar air
And dropped white petals on his hair.

James Wright

A Presentation of Two Birds to My Son

Chicken. How shall I tell you what it is,
And why it does not float with tanagers?
Its ecstasy is dead, it does not care.
Its children huddle underneath its wings,
And altogether lounge against the shack,
Warm in the slick tarpaulin, smug and soft.

You must not fumble in your mind
The genuine ecstasy of climbing birds
With that dull fowl.
When your grandfather held it by the feet
And laid the skinny neck across
The ragged chopping block,
The flop of wings, the jerk of the red comb
Were a dumb agony,
Stupid and meaningless. It was no joy

To leave the body beaten underfoot;
Life was a flick of corn, a steady roost.
Chicken. The sound is plain.

Look up and see the swift above the trees.
How shall I tell you why he always veers
And banks around the shaken sleeve of air,
Away from ground? He hardly flies on brains;
Pockets of air impale his hollow bones.
He leans against the rainfall or the sun.

You must not mix this pair of birds
Together in your mind before you know
That both are clods.
What makes the chimney swift approach the sky
Is ecstasy, a kind of fire
That beats the bones apart
And lets the fragile feathers close the air.
Flight too is agony,
Stupid and meaningless. Why should it be joy
To leave the body beaten underfoot,
To mold the limbs against the wind, and join
Those clean dark glides of Dionysian birds?
The flight is deeper than your father, boy.

James Wright

Youth

Strange bird,
His song remains secret.
He worked too hard to read books.

163

He never heard how Sherwood Anderson
Got out of it, and fled to Chicago, furious to free himself
From his hatred of factories.
My father toiled fifty years
At Hazel-Atlas Glass,
Caught among girders that smash the kneecaps
Of dumb honyaks.
Did he shudder with hatred in the cold shadow of grease?
Maybe. But my brother and I do know
He came home as quiet as the evening.

He will be getting dark, soon,
And loom through new snow.
I know his ghost will drift home
To the Ohio River, and sit down, alone,
Whittling a root.
He will say nothing.
The waters flow past, older, younger
Than he is, or I am.

Donald Hall

Christmas Eve in Whitneyville
To my father

December, and the closing of the year;
The momentary carolers complete
Their Christmas Eves, and quickly disappear
Into their houses on each lighted street.

Each car is put away in each garage;
Each husband home from work, to celebrate,

Has closed his house around him like a cage,
And wedged the tree until the tree stood straight.

Tonight you lie in Whitneyville again,
Near where you lived, and near the woods or farms
Which Eli Whitney settled with the men
Who worked at mass-producing firearms.

The main-street, which was nothing after all
Except a school, a stable, and two stores,
Was improvised and individual,
Picking its way alone, until the wars.

Now Whitneyville is like the other places,
Ranch-houses stretching flat beyond the square,
Same stores and movie, same composite faces
Speaking the language of the public air.

Old buildings loiter by this cemetery.
When you were twelve, they dressed you up in black
With five companions from the class, to carry
The body of a friend. Now you are back,

Beside him, but a man of fifty-two.
Talk to the boy. Tell him about the years
When Whitneyville quadrupled, and how you
And all his friends went on to make careers,

Had cars as long as hayricks, boarded planes,
For Rome and Paris where the pace was slow,
And took the time to think how yearly gains,
Profit and volume made the business grow.

"The things you had to miss," you said last week,
"Or thought you had to, take your breath away."
You propped yourself on pillows, where your cheek
Was hollow, stubbled lightly with new gray.

This love is jail; another sets us free.
Tonight the houses and their noise distort

The thin rewards of solidarity.
The houses lean together for support.

The noises fail. Now lights go on upstairs.
The men and women are undressing now
To go to sleep. They put their clothes on chairs
To take them up again. I think of how,

Across America, when midnight comes,
They lie together and are quieted,
To sleep as children sleep, who suck their thumbs,
Cramped in the narrow rumple of each bed.

They will not have unpleasant thoughts tonight.
They make their houses jails, and they will take
No risk of freedom for the appetite,
Or knowledge of it, when they are awake.

The lights go out and it is Christmas Day.
The stones are white, the grass is black and deep;
I will go back and leave you here to stay,
While the dark houses harden into sleep.

Donald Hall

My Son, My Executioner

My son, my executioner,
   I take you in my arms,
Quiet and small and just astir,
   And whom my body warms.

Sweet death, small son, our instrument
   Of immortality,

Your cries and hungers document
   Our bodily decay.

We twenty-five and twenty-two,
   Who seemed to live forever,
Observe enduring life in you
   And start to die together.

Philip Levine

My Son and I

In a coffee house at 3 am
and he believes
I'm dying. Outside the wind
moves along the streets
of New York City picking up
abandoned scraps of newspapers
and tiny messages of hope
no one hears. He's dressed
in worn corduroy pants
and shirts over shirts,
and his hands are stained
as mine once were
with glue, ink, paint.
A brown stocking cap
hides the thick blond hair
so unlike mine. For forty
minutes he's tried not
to cry. How are his brothers?
I tell him I don't know,
they have grown away

from me. We are Americans
and never touch on this
stunned earth where a boy
sees his life fly past
through a car window. His mother?
She is deaf and works
in the earth for days, hearing
the dirt pray and guiding
the worm to its feasts. Why
do I have to die? Why
do I have to sit before him
no longer his father, only
a man? Because the given
must be taken, because
we hunger before we eat,
because each small spark
must turn to darkness.
As we said when we were kids
and knew the names of everything
...just because. I reach
across the table and take
his left hand in mine.
I have no blessing. I can
tell him how I found
the plum blossom before
I was thirty, how once
in a rooming house in Alicante
a man younger than I,
an Argentine I barely understood,
sat by me through the night
while my boy Teddy cried out
for help, and how when he slept
at last, my friend wept
with thanks in the cold light.
I can tell him that his hand

sweating in mine can raise
the Lord God of Stones,
bring down the Republic of Lies,
and hold a spoon. Instead
I say it's late, and he pays
and leads me back
through the empty streets
to the Earl Hotel, where
the room sours with the mould
of old Bibles dumped down
the air-shaft. In my coat
I stand alone in the dark
waiting for something,
a flash of light, a song,
a remembered sweetness
from all the lives I've lost.
Next door the TV babbles
on and on, and I give up
and sway toward the bed
in a last chant before dawn.

Philip Levine

The Face

A strange wind off the night.
I have come here to talk
to you at last, here
in an empty hotel room
half the world away from home.
Our tracks have crossed

how many times—a dozen
at least—and yet it's more
than forty years since I saw
you, solemn and hurt, gazing
from your favorite window
at the night that would
soon flood your eyes and darken
the living veins. Below,
the city is almost
asleep. An old man, no
taller than a boy, mumbles
drunkenly on his way,
and then only a sentry
passes from time to time,
his head sunk to his chest,
his eyes closed against
the strange summer cold.

We should all be asleep.
The hour is good for
nothing else, and yet
I cannot sleep because
suddenly today I caught
your presence beside me
on the street as I hadn't
before in all these years.
A tall man laid aside
his paper and stared at me,
a man no older than I,
with the long, sad face
that passed from you
to me. I kept walking,
feeling his eyes on me,
and when I turned at last
he was gone and the bench
filled with dirty children.

I went back—but no—
he was gone, and wherever
I walked I felt those eyes
on me and felt somehow
a time had come when
we might speak at last.

And so I do. I say, Father,
the years have brought
me here, still your son;
they have brought me
to a life I cannot
understand. I'm silent.
A ship is mooring
in the great harbor,
and the only voice
that comes back is the faint
after-ringing of my own.
I say, Father, the dark
must once have guided you
across the twelve frontiers
you crossed to save
your life. It leads me
nowhere, for I'm a free man,
alone as you were,
but going nowhere. I, too,
have lost my three sons
to America, I, too, have climbed
the long hillsides
of Spain in early light
as our forefathers did,
and gazed down at the sea,
deep and silent. I prayed
for some small hope,
which never came. I know
the life you lost. I

have it here, Father,
where you left it, in
the long face of Spain,
in these hands, long
and broken like your own,
in the silence collecting
between each ringing
of my heart, the silence
you anoint me with each day.

Below, the sentry passes
once more in a new light,
for morning is graying
the streets of this quarter.
He wipes his nose on
the rough green wool
of his sleeve and stamps
his feet. Spain will waken
soon to street cries, to
the cries of children,
the cries of the lost men
and women of Barcelona
naming their despair.
I will walk among them,
tired and useless. Today
I will not talk, not
even to myself, for
it is time to listen,
as though some secret
message came blaring
over the megaphones,
or a voice mumbled below
the waves of traffic, as though
one word mattered more
than another in this world,
in this city, broken and stained,

which is the home of no one,
though it shouts out all
our names. I will listen
as though you spoke and told
me all you never knew
of why the earth takes
back all she gives and
even that comes to be enough.

L.E. Sissman

Going Home, 1945
(Part II. At Home)

2. The Folks

My father casts a stone whose ripples ride
Almost to my unhearing aid, the ear.
My answering fire likewise falls short. Between
Us lies no-generation's land, a waste
Of time. Barbed wire and trenches separate
The conscript class of 1895
From that of 1928. I see
My father, in a tall examination room
Gaslit by fishtail burners, demonstrate
The differential calculus; he sees
Me boozing with low types in Central Square
And touching tasty women on the quick.
(Not such a bad idea, Dad, after all.)
Had he his way, his little mathemat
Would be devouring sums and public praise

Like any Univac; and had I mine,
My dad and I would be out on the town,
Like as a brother act in our black ties,
Clubbable, bibulous, sly, debonair.
Fat chance of that. Across the timing gap
No blue spark fires. We talk in circles which
Are not contiguous. It is too bad
Our purposes for others founder on
Their purposes for us. Now, take my dad.

L.E. Sissman

Parents in Winter
(Part II. Father at Packard's, 1915)

The brick plant like a school. The winter set
Of East Grand Boulevard. The violets
Of dawn relent to let us see the first
Shift of its students hurrying to class
Distinction in the undistinguished mass
Concealing offices and cubicles,
Great drawing rooms with draftsmen on their stools,
Foremen's rude cabins bringing outdoors in,
Craftsmen's workbenches littered with their trim
Brushes and colors, and, in Main, the lines
Of workers in their hundreds vanishing,
With our perspective, at the end of all
The crucial stations in their longsome hall.
Here comes my father. Look how thin he is.
See snowflakes flower on the blank plat of his
Forehead. Note his black hair. In hand,

He has already all the instruments
(Pre-war and German in their provenance)
To tap and die a life. Intolerant
To the last thousandth, they encompass all
Protracted elevations of his soul,
And in their narrow ink lines circumscribe
The isometric renderings of pride
Which will propel him through the glacial years
While he designs the sun and planet gears.

L.E. Sissman

Tras os montes
II. Father (1895-1974)

Whether the rivals for a wife and mother can
Compose their differences and timely warp
Into concomitant currents, taken by
Of melting in the middle of the night—
Is to be seen. We did not find it so.
My father, whom I loved as if he'd done
All his devoirs (though he had not), and shone
Upon my forehead like a morning sun,
Came home out of his hospital to stay
In our rich, alien house, where trappings tried
His niggard monkishness. Four days he stayed
In his ashen cocoon; the fifth he died
Under my ministrations, his pug jaw
Thrust out toward the port of hopelessness,
Where he (I hope) received the sirens of

All possible welcoming tugs, even as I
Felt under his grey, waxen nose for breath
And called the doctor to record a death
That made shift rather easier for me,
Staring at nothing standing out to sea.

John Hollander

Tales Told of the Fathers

1 THE MOMENT
In a cold glade sacred to nothing
He stood waiting, withholding his gaze
From unquestioned sky, unanswering
Grass, he later supposed, all the while
Growing unfelt beneath his bared soles.
The sky was not green although the grass
Was gray, and he felt the moment pass,
With no breath, when some ten of them might
Have come whispering through the dark brush,
Past spaces of water and beyond
Regions of erased shapes in the air,
To conduct him far away on foot
To a place not of earth, but only
Of abominations: dirt and soil,
Shit and mud mingling in wet trenches,
Where he would have stood bound and retching,
Aghast, but of course unsurprised as
Soundlessly the things were done, as then
The trembling foal dropped into a vat
Of rotten wine, the kid fell forward

Into the seething milk—but the wind
Breathed for him; the moment came and went
For the thin ten that time. He could wait.

2   THE PICTURES
His reflection in water said:
The father is light's general,
The son is but a morning star
Whose every rising into the
Failure of daylight makes the great
Case of upward fall—O see him
Bleaching out in the high morning!
His cold shadow on the rock said:
Under me, unshading, lies the
Skeleton of an Indian.
The dead. The dead are not even
Things. No odd beings. Stones and bones
Fall away to bone and stone then
To crumbling, then to part of night.

3   A CUP OF TREMBLINGS
Facing deep wine raised in the
Tilted, earthen cup, the dark
Opening into further
Dark, eyes wide, he could perceive,
Around the rim of the dark,
Breathings of the afternoon;
As, eyes shuttered, he could see
Sleep, so, opened, they would show
Him death—but now momently
In the heart of the wine, far
Away, the muses of waltz
Moved, as if seen from a height
Down a narrowing defile,
In an unshadowed meadow.

4   THE SIGN

When he saw a skull floating
On the face of the waters
With a mind of air and eyes
Of wind, it was not a sign
Of drowning generations
Themselves now drowned. It was no
Mere wonder of mirroring,
But part of the garbage of
Pain, the usual offal
Of encounter: a fallen
Top of something no choiring
Winds' melismata question,
The dark, hollow shard of a
Vessel of decreated
Clay, a cup of life emptied.

—And seeing it just at noon,
Bobbing on bright water at
The most transparent time, when
He could look back over his
Shoulder and see a clear field,
When his long, ever-vengeful
Shadow vanishes and stops,
For a moment, following:
This was most dreadful of all.

5   THE GARDEN

High on his brick cliff his garden hung
Open eastward and backed against the
Heights that hid the broad, showy deathbed
Of the sun, whose Tiepolo gestures
He read raving reviews of in the
Fiery mirrors of the west-watching
Windows set in other distant cliffs.
It was there that he muttered about

His pots of spiky dill and broad mint,
His borders of concealing privet.
Edenist of the mid-air, he gazed
At the black oily kernels of dust
Flung as if by some high sower and
Languidly fallen through the forenoon
Over the walls, mingling with his soil.
He had had to make do among smut
And fruitless grit; had lopped and pruned all
The branches of shadow and with care
Hung the leathern mock-adder among
His greens to scare grumbling doves away.
In the evening cool his dull cigar
Breathed and glowed. This was all that there was
To keep. And there was nothing to lose.

Robert Pack

The Boat

I dressed my father in his little clothes,
Blue sailor suit, brass buttons on his coat.
He asked me where the running water goes.

"Down to the sea," I said; "Set it afloat!"
Beside the stream he bent and raised the sail,
Uncurled the string and launched the painted boat.

White birds, circling the mast, wrenched his eyes pale.
He leaped on the tight deck and took the wind.
I watched the ship foam lurching in the gale,

And cried, "Come back, you don't know what you'll find!"
He steered. The ship grew, reddening the sky
As waves throbbed back, blind stumbling after blind.

The storm receded in his darkened eyes,
And down he looked at me. A harbor rose.
I asked, "What happens, father, when you die?"

He told where all the running water goes,
And dressed me gently in my little clothes.

Milton Kessler

The Sea's Last Gift: 1961

1

Wonderful weather!
The pain of yes
and something beginning:
Two forms whimper at a pond's edge;
a wild rose brims with yearning, spills;
seed and tendril swell;
the winds caress an embryo's dilation;
and cool in the green musk of dawn
she turns, woeful as an injured dancer,
a lily in her first fondling,
to a naked boy
tremulous with knowing.

O wonderful wonderful!
Yet too wonderful....

A bloodstain desecrates an egg.
Her breast removed, the cell panics;
her mind dies, the soul's aftermath.
And the other one (thorns are my eyes),
must he ever be a cart for stones?
O brother of Job,
has time a father,
are all fallings graveward?

Softly. It is not your universe.
Your family wants; the beach is ready.
Go to the water. Reason. Rest.

2

Your family wants, your family, your.
An ailing pedant I have walked these walls,
a moth alone in a dream's projection.
My skull's three ages breathe apart,
each for its wound, its shape of sky, its lover.
It weeps. Which child am I? Perhaps? Try?
Inflate a balloon. Cradle your face against it.
A heaviness rises, trembles my sill...
O mother of union, I fall! I fall!

3

When I came out
into blessings of salt air
it was a painter's morning.
The beach had a bowl's truth.
Here my child created valleys,
my wife combed herself a girl;
and (the sea's last gift)
Macy shirt wind-swelled to a hump,
chewing the frizzled stump
of his Phillies,

my vacationing father,
in lisle socks
and night-shift pallor,
fighting sand, the gull
of his World-Telegram,
the rash of Indian summer,
was irritable, alien,
off-season in a rented beach-chair.

Robert Winner

Elegy

I remember the feel of a hammer—
its grainy handle placing
its head's steel weight in your palm,
or the rung of a ladder
pressing confidently into your foot,
or how the sun felt on your skin, or cold water
as it dissolved the wall of salt
at the back of your throat.

I remember how you sang in your stone shoes
light-voiced as dusk or feathers,
how your shoes turned outward again—
as they used to when you walked—
when you lay in your dead body on the floor
and showed us the shining nail-heads
around each earth-scuffed leather sole.

Gary Snyder

The Bath

Washing Kai in the sauna,
The kerosene lantern set on a box
   outside the ground-level window,
Lights up the edge of the iron stove and the
   washtub down on the slab
Steaming air and crackle of waterdrops
   brushed by on the pile of rocks on top
He stands in warm water
Soap all over the smooth of his thigh and stomach
   "Gary don't soap my hair!"
   —his eye-sting fear—
   the soapy hand feeling
   through and around the globes and curves of his body,
   up in the crotch,
And washing-tickling out the scrotum, little anus,
   his penis curving up and getting hard
   as I pull back skin and try to wash it
Laughing and jumping, flinging arms around,
   I squat all naked too,
                is this our body?

Sweating and panting in the stove-steam hot-stone
   cedar-planking wooden bucket water-splashing
   kerosene lantern-flicker wind-in-the-pines-out
   sierra forest ridges night—
Masa comes in, letting fresh cool air
   sweep down from the door
   a deep sweet breath
And she tips him over gripping neatly, one knee down
   her hair falling hiding one whole side of
   shoulder, breast, and belly,
Washes deftly Kai's head-hair
   as he gets mad and yells—

The body of my lady, the winding valley spine,
    the space between the thighs I reach through,
    cup her curving vulva arch and hold it from behind,
    a soapy tickle   a hand of grail
The gates of Awe
That open back a turning double-mirror world of
    wombs in wombs, in rings,
    that start in music,
                    is this our body?

The hidden place of seed
The veins net flow across the ribs, that gathers
    milk and peaks up in a nipple—fits
    our mouth—
The sucking milk from this our body sends through
    jolts of light; the son, the father,
    sharing mother's joy
That brings a softness to the flower of the awesome
    open curling lotus gate I cup and kiss
As Kai laughs at his mother's breast he now is weaned
    from, we
    wash each other,
                    this our body

Kai's little scrotum up close to his groin,
    the seed still tucked away, that moved from us to him
In flows that lifted with the same joys forces
    as his nursing Masa later,
    playing with her breast,
Or me within her,
Or him emerging,
                    this is our body:

Clean, and rinsed, and sweating more, we stretch
    out on the redwood benches hearts all beating

Quiet to the simmer of the stove,
      the scent of cedar
And then turn over,
      murmuring gossip of the grasses,
      talking firewood,
Wondering how Gen's napping, how to bring him in
      soon wash him too—
These boys who love their mother
      who loves men, who passes on
      her sons to other women;

The cloud across the sky. The windy pines.
      the trickle gurgle in the swampy meadow

      this is our body.

Fire inside and boiling water on the stove
We sigh and slide ourselves down from the benches
      wrap the babies, step outside,

black night & all the stars.

Pour cold water on the back and thighs
Go in the house—stand steaming by the center fire
Kai scampers on the sheepskin
Gen standing hanging on and shouting,

"Bao!   bao!   bao!   bao!   bao!"

This is our body. Drawn up crosslegged by the flames
      drinking icy water
      hugging babies, kissing bellies,

Laughing on the Great Earth

Come out from the bath.

Etheridge Knight

The Bones of My Father

There are no dry bones
here in this valley. The skull
of my father grins
at the Mississippi moon
from the bottom
of the Tallahatchie,
the bones of my father
are buried in the mud
of these creeks and brooks that twist
and flow their secrets to the sea.
but the wind sings to me
here the sun speaks to me
of the dry bones of my father.

2

There are no dry bones
in the northern valleys, in the Harlem alleys
young/black/men with knees bent
nod on the stoops of the tenements
and dream
of the dry bones of my father.

And young white longhairs who flee
their homes, and bend their minds
and sing their songs of brotherhood
and no more wars are searching for
my father's bones.

3

There are no dry bones
here, my brothers. We hide from the sun.
No more do we take the long straight strides.
Our steps have been shaped by the cages

that kept us. We glide sideways
like crabs across the sand.
We perch on green lilies, we search
beneath white rocks....
THERE ARE NO DRY BONES HERE

The skull of my father
grins at the Mississippi moon
from the bottom
of the Tallahatchie.

Conn.—Feb. 21, 1971

Etheridge Knight

On the Birth of a Black/Baby/Boy
(for Isaac BuShie Blackburn-Knight)

In Memphis—in Tennessee.
(O Come—and go / wid / meeee...)
In Memphis, in Tennessee—
In the year of (y) our Lord, 1978—
             (and the christian / suicides in Guyana).
In the bubbles and the blood of Boss Crump's guilt—
In the blueness of the hospitality of his / hos / pi / tal—
In the sterile gowns, green and growing—
In Memphis, in Tennessee...

Where all women / are / whining Queens,
Where black walnuts drop like leaves,
Where all women / are / shining Queens—
Where / cops / act / much worse than the thieves—

In Memphis, in Tennessee...

When / the blood of your birth / is / screaming forth
                              like a fountain
                                           from
                              the white thighs of your mother—
When / her / hand / is / tight on mine—
When I sink in / side her belly, and cling to / you—
When / short miles to the south the Ku Klux / Klan
                              march like locusts over / this / land-
When mayors / like Moscone / are / shot down, like
                              Martin, Malcolm, and Medgar Ever
When Jimmy Carter / tries / to *stand* where Martin *stood*
In Memphis, in Tennessee—And.

As the lady / medic / with her long black hair
                    taunts your mother: O push push push *pu*

As / my / belly / becomes a drum and my blood beseech thee-
As / my / heart / becomes a song and my eyes lakes of lightni
As / your / mother grunts for 3 / days and groans for 3 / nigh
As / she issues you / forth on a sunday night,
                    (on a chilling, raining, sun / day / nigl
                    and now.
As you lay warming in my arms, son—
                    all I/can/say son, is:
You / be a loonngg time coming, boy—
But you're wel / come here.

                                        November—December

David Ray

At the Washing of My Son
to Samuel

I ran up and grabbed your arm, the way a man
On a battlefield would recognize a long lost comrade.
You were still wrinkled, and had a hidden face
Like a hedgehog or a mouse, and you crouched in
The black elbows of a Negro nurse. You were
Covered with your mother's blood, and I saw
That navel where you and I were joined to her.
I stood by the glass and watched you squeal.
Just twice in a man's life there's this
Scrubbing off of blood. And this holy
Rite that Mother Superior in her white starched hat
Was going to deny me. But I stood my ground.
And then went in where for the first time you saw
Your mother's face, and her open blouse.

Amiri Baraka

The Ballgame.

We road the hiways
from our loways
going a ways from home, up the 21 road
to see a baseball game
my son was (supposed) to be
in.

It was dusk like a songing smell, abrupt
its lips sucking dirt and swirling it

among animals and people with their backs
turned. What can I say the weeds like words
scattering under the bellies of
birds, our record players
linking us to
hot history

Not a busload, but checkered stragglers
abandoning for a minute, the alcoholic streets of gray Nwk.

Oh, there is green, out there where even some not even rich
white
folks
live. More parks in those few blocks than all
of our town. (A bird, larking, tennis wing shadows
brightness
whispering

                           The score surged back
& forth, the white boys won
& their rascally colored
friends
Can you all ways make it afternoon?

Our talk and laughter
surges
back & forth, the funny wind
batting
its
eyes

Our kids ran, and got
mad: They got some hits
and slid, and scored

This aint even a very slick neighborhood
but money talks
and we could rarely

get a walk
but we kept walking
them.
   The brother meanwhile talked of Gibson
& other
      nuts, & what happened to you
      (about the killer cops)

      & asked your reporter
      to run
      for mayor

that wdnt work, we'll get
someone
      until the white boys
      hd scored bunches of runs and led
      11 to 6, going into
   the last inning.

            We had had bravado
            & noise, in stretches
         even up in the not even woods
      our sons had tears
   in their eyes/at the end
  taught white supremacy, the hard way
a stadium, with announcer, groundkeeper, and electric
scoreboard—

unable to be spared that
even on a cool bright day
even by the middleclass negro
who heads up our league
or his wife, who coaches
our tiny all stars
or their son
who plays,
second base

none of these
cd help much
their
message

((is it an sos in bubbles
  you know, an un-coola

is it the tears of little boys
like mine, who did not even
play, and brought half their tribe up
to see, they know they can
        the message, out there just beyond Newark
        where it aint even got good yet
        the dark brown woman passed the bottle
        thru her brother to me
        and we let em know who we cared
        about—they were our children
        we gonna raise em
        we gonna help em
        this ain the end

        she was holding her own tears back
        I aint done much with my
        life, walking away with us
        her son was starting pitcher
        got knocked/out the box
    you see she was telling us about the case
    I want to help, and you all come to dinner
    chicken and greens, get down afroamerican style
    I've got to do something, you know, to make things
    better, for my children (the kids were hanging their head

but they'll come back
we all wanted to say
like the sun does
and we stood and talked, and managed laughs
like we do, anyway, until
the kids

came

we'll see you
we hoped we would
like the strength we exchanged
we know its real

& then back
on the hiways
would yall but understand
the orchestration of the situation
the machinations in hi stations the scum that control
the wealth
of the
nation

Our little boys tears
are enough
dont you think. Their hot disgust
that they cd be beaten/by white
boys
like they had dollar bills
for bats
& grins banging
like cash
registers

It is enough, all you different kind of negroes
& colored people
you afro americans, and black afternoon blue tinged
singers
& laborers
it is enough, meaning, catch what light there is as you wave
& hug the little dudes just a split second
close
if you cd teach them, reality, so their eyes wd dry and fly
open the future, you know
wd be, hpper than this...much much hipper

Stephen Berg

For My Father

At the Door

Black trees. The banks fill with shadow.
Where the roadlamps throw their blue light
on the water, it's alive.
We drive by without speaking.
Everything is so peaceful outside,
and inside, that the deep endless laugh
of a man who has found happiness begins
and I remember my daughters coming up to me
and smiling, saying whatever they wanted to
without fear.
This is enough. Give everything else
to the hungry.
They say each person has a story
but that's not true.
We live.
The leaves are so dark tonight I can't see them
but I feel them breathe,
the river's moving on but all I see
are wrinkled patches of blue light, squirming.
My father's dying.
He's asleep now next to my mother as the car plows through.
She sits and waits.
I stick my arm out the window
and let it be a wing.
I know what to do.

To the Same Place

The first warm summer afternoon I ask my friend
to ride out with his two daughters and me.
We park by the river.
Everybody's there, cooking, dozing, biking,

playing ball. We get out and look for shade
and sit under a huge cherry tree.
I envy the steady unpredictable growth
that has taken everything and survived,
I pick at the tiny lumps that have pushed through
the papery brownish-pink bark that glows.
Then, knowing there's no escape from grief,
I pick up the whiffle ball and we catch—
curves, knucklers, floaters, anything we can
get going on the clear air, and slowly again
the peace I felt
when we drove past this place nights ago
spreads through me.
Now his children crawl on the low branches, screaming.
They jump down and scoop handfuls of parched dirt
and carry it to us.
                    How much is left?
The dusty grains flare out through their fingers
and Jeff points out how small the young cherries are
this early, not ready to eat,
and squeezes one
until its juice stains his fingers.
The branch snaps back.
The children want to eat them.
That's how it is, wanting to eat green cherries,
getting sick. But fathers protect us,
we think, until they die.
Then we stand on the earth
in front of our children, fathers ourselves,
and the bitter taste of love sings on our tongues.

Driving Out Again At Night

A full moon tilts over the lawns and trees.
Pale shadows, pockets of heat,
couples humped along the riverbanks,

these and the invisible road cure me.
The arclights are out for miles.
I still carry you inside me, Dad, one hundred
and thirteen extra pounds, gray-faced and weak,
but out here the smell
of water and leaves fills me and pushes you out.
I'm sorry. I love you. But I have to let you go.
So we drive away again
into a few blurred things,
my friend and I, talking.
When cars rush by us they blind me
and I like not seeing. We turn left
over the bridge to come back
and a couple dances across the road, caught
in our beams, the boy holding a brown
paper bag with a bottle in it.
Its mouth flashes.
On my left the river is as clear as a baby's eyes.
When I look toward the stretches of grass, soaked in darkne
sweeping by, I see myself twenty years ago
lying there with a girl
and pound the dashboard with my fist.
Back in the city
the lights on floor after floor of offices stay on.
Nobody's there. The last
shoppers pause at the frozen bodies that shine
in store windows then straggle home
to a silence nothing explains.

Red Weed

next to me on the riverbank,
I pluck you out of the dirt,
I hold you
between two fingers
because I'm alone.

I wish I could speak through the invisible
roots I have,
not through my face.
You don't have a face,
brown roots going nowhere,
bloody spiked crown.
When I toss you
you sail a few inches
then fall onto the water
and drift away.
There's my father the morning I woke
and saw him. I see him
in me, eyes
open, mouth open,
drifting away.
He didn't wake.
The spot of blood he coughed up on the pillow's
you, red weed,
so tiny, so clear when I held you
up against the sky, so
wise not to answer, god
of the box of ashes,
father.

Mark Strand

Elegy for My Father
(Robert Strand 1908–68)

1   The Empty Body

The hands were yours, the arms were yours,
But you were not there.

The eyes were yours, but they were closed and would not o
The distant sun was there.
The moon poised on the hill's white shoulder was there.
The wind on Bedford Basin was there.
The pale green light of winter was there.
Your mouth was there,
But you were not there.
When somebody spoke, there was no answer.
Clouds came down
And buried the buildings along the water,
And the water was silent.
The gulls stared.
The years, the hours, that would not find you
Turned in the wrists of others.
There was no pain. It had gone.
There were no secrets. There was nothing to say.
The shade scattered its ashes.
The body was yours, but you were not there.
The air shivered against its skin.
The dark leaned into its eyes.
But you were not there.

2   *Answers*

Why did you travel?
Because the house was cold.
Why did you travel?
Because it is what I have always done between sunset and sunrise.
What did you wear?
I wore a blue suit, a white shirt, yellow tie, and yellow socks.
What did you wear?
I wore nothing. A scarf of pain kept me warm.
Who did you sleep with?
I slept with a different woman each night.
Who did you sleep with?
I slept alone. I have always slept alone.

198

Why did you lie to me?
I always thought I told the truth.
Why did you lie to me?
Because the truth lies like nothing else and I love the truth.
Why are you going?
Because nothing means much to me anymore.
Why are you going?
I don't know. I have never known.
How long shall I wait for you?
Do not wait for me. I am tired and I want to lie down.
Are you tired and do you want to lie down?
Yes, I am tired and I want to lie down.

3   *Your Dying*

Nothing could stop you.
Not the best day. Not the quiet. Not the ocean rocking.
You went on with your dying.
Not the trees
Under which you walked, not the trees that shaded you.
Not the doctor
Who warned you, the white-haired young doctor who saved you once.
You went on with your dying.
Nothing could stop you. Not your son. Not your daughter
Who fed you and made you into a child again.
Not your son who thought you would live forever.
Not the wind that shook your lapels.
Not the stillness that offered itself to your motion.
Not your shoes that grew heavier.
Not your eyes that refused to look ahead.
Nothing could stop you.
You sat in your room and stared at the city
And went on with your dying.
You went to work and let the cold enter your clothes.
You let blood seep into your socks.

Your face turned white.
Your voice cracked in two.
You leaned on your cane.
But nothing could stop you.
Not your friends who gave you advice.
Not your son. Not your daughter who watched you grow sm
Not fatigue that lived in your sighs.
Not your lungs that would fill with water.
Not your sleeves that carried the pain of your arms.
Nothing could stop you.
You went on with your dying.
When you played with children you went on with your dying
When you sat down to eat,
When you woke up at night, wet with tears, your body sobbi
You went on with your dying.
Nothing could stop you.
Not the past.
Not the future with its good weather.
Not the view from your window, the view of the graveyard.
Not the city. Not the terrible city with its wooden buildings.
Not defeat. Not success.
You did nothing but go on with your dying.
You put your watch to your ear.
You felt yourself slipping.
You lay on the bed.
You folded your arms over your chest and you dreamed of t
    world without you,
Of the space under the trees,
Of the space in your room,
Of the spaces that would now be empty of you,
And you went on with your dying.
Nothing could stop you.
Not your breathing. Not your life.
Not the life you wanted.
Not the life you had.
Nothing could stop you.

You have your shadow.
The places where you were have given it back.
The hallways and bare lawns of the orphanage have given it
      back.
The Newsboys Home has given it back.
The streets of New York have given it back and so have the
      streets of Montreal.
The rooms in Belém where lizards would snap at mosquitos have
      given it back.
The dark streets of Manaus and the damp streets of Rio have
      given it back.
Mexico City where you wanted to leave it has given it back.
And Halifax where the harbor would wash its hands of you has
      given it back.
You have your shadow.
When you traveled the white wake of your going sent your
      shadow below, but when you arrived it was there to greet you.
      You had your shadow.
The doorways you entered lifted your shadow from you and
      when you went out, gave it back. You had your shadow.
Even when you forgot your shadow, you found it again; it had
      been with you.
Once in the country the shade of a tree covered your shadow and
      you were not known.
Once in the country you thought your shadow had been cast by
      somebody else. Your shadow said nothing.
Your clothes carried your shadow inside; when you took them
      off, it spread like the dark of your past.
And your words that float like leaves in an air that is lost, in a
      place no one knows, gave you back your shadow.
Your friends gave you back your shadow.
Your enemies gave you back your shadow. They said it was
      heavy and would cover your grave.

When you died your shadow slept at the mouth of the furn.
    and ate ashes for bread.
It rejoiced among ruins.
It watched while others slept.
It shone like crystal among the tombs.
It composed itself like air.
It wanted to be like snow on water.
It wanted to be nothing, but that was not possible.
It came to my house.
It sat on my shoulders.
Your shadow is yours. I told it so. I said it was yours.
I have carried it with me too long. I give it back.

5   *Mourning*

They mourn for you.
When you rise at midnight,
And the dew glitters on the stone of your cheeks,
They mourn for you.
They lead you back into the empty house.
They carry the chairs and tables inside.
They sit you down and teach you to breathe.
And your breath burns,
It burns the pine box and the ashes fall like sunlight.
They give you a book and tell you to read.
They listen and their eyes fill with tears.
The women stroke your fingers.
They comb the yellow back into your hair.
They shave the frost from your beard.
They knead your thighs.
They dress you in fine clothes.
They rub your hands to keep them warm.
They feed you. They offer you money.
They get on their knees and beg you not to die.
When you rise at midnight they mourn for you.
They close their eyes and whisper your name over and over.

But they cannot drag the buried light from your veins.
They cannot reach your dreams.
Old man, there is no way.
Rise and keep rising, it does no good.
They mourn for you the way they can.

6 The New Year

It is winter and the new year.
Nobody knows you.
Away from the stars, from the rain of light,
You lie under the weather of stones.
There is no thread to lead you back.
Your friends doze in the dark
Of pleasure and cannot remember.
Nobody knows you. You are the neighbor of nothing.
You do not see the rain falling and the man walking away,
The soiled wind blowing its ashes across the city.
You do not see the sun dragging the moon like an echo.
You do not see the bruised heart go up in flames,
The skulls of the innocent turn into smoke.
You do not see the scars of plenty, the eyes without light.
It is over. It is winter and the new year.
The meek are hauling their skins into heaven.
The hopeless are suffering the cold with those who have nothing
    to hide.
It is over and nobody knows you.
There is starlight drifting on the black water.
There are stones in the sea no one has seen.
There is a shore and people are waiting.
And nothing comes back.
Because it is over.
Because there is silence instead of a name.
Because it is winter and the new year.

Laurence Lieberman

Lamb and Bear: Jet Landing
(for Isaac)

At each level
of jetfall, rougher turbulence:
    my son, in deepest
slumber of engine-drone, drug-limbed,
    nods. I motion to undo
his belt, hesitate . . . *a wind-gust*
    could send you flying,
loose egg, across the cabin. . . .

When you awake,
if you wish, you can cut me
    in twos, in two
halves, or two mes, your dreamed
    sirs, so gladly
beside you, shining. Do you know,
    my shut lips, if they
could tell, glow. Inside, I am

who opens up to you.
Unsticking your eyelids, sleep's
    fleece sheering off,
you look at my hands, then yours.
    You concentrate. Soon,
we've exchanged hands, yours
    doubled, mine halved.
You look up—we trade faces,

not eyes. My son,
if it please you, enter.
    Lean into my
bones. Slide under my skin.
    Wear me. An old
bear hide, hairy, pot-bellied.
    When I wither (I
promise I shall), shed me!

Robert Mezey

One Summer

My father coming home
from the factory
summer and still light out
the green bus at the end
of the endless street
the foul sigh
on which my father stepped down
walking slowly in the shadows
holding my hand
my father tired and frowning
eating his supper of potatoes
reading the *Bulletin*
news of the war
and columns of boxscores
my father singing lewd hymns
in his tuneless voice
stretched out full length in the tub
his calves hanging over the rim
his long penis resting
on the surface of the grey water

Charles Wright

Firstborn
—*Omnia quae sunt, lumina sunt*—

1

The sugar dripping into your vein;
The jaundice rising upon your face like a blush;

The glass box they keep you in—

The bandage over your eyes;
The curdled milk on your lips;
The plastic tube in your throat—

The unseen hands that linger against your skin;
The name, like a new scar, at your wrist;
The glass box they keep you in—

We bring what we have to bring;
We give what we have to give;
Welcome, sweet Luke, to your life.

2

The bougainvillaea's redress
Pulses throughout the hillside, its slow
Network of vines

Holding the earth together, giving it breath;
Outside your window, hibiscus and columbine
Tend to their various needs;

The summer enlarges.
                              You, too, enlarge,
Becoming accessible,
Your liquid reshufflings

Protracted and ill defined,
Yet absolute after all, the new skin
Blossoming pink and clear.

3

You lie here beside me now,
Ineffable, elsewhere still.
What should one say to a son?

Emotions and points of view, the large
Abstractions we like to think
We live by—or would live by if things

Were other than what they are;
Or we were; or others were;
If all were altered and more distinct?

Or something immediate,
Descriptive, the virtuous use of words?
What can one say to a son?

4

If it were possible, if
A way had been overlooked
To pull that rib of pure light

Out of its cage, those few felicitous vowels
Which expiate everything...
But nothing has been left out,

Nothing been overlooked.
The words remain in the dark, and will
Continue to glitter there;

No tricks we try to invent,
No strategies, can now extract them.
And dust is dust for a long time.

5

What I am trying to say
Is this—I tell you, only, the thing
That I have come to believe:

Indenture yourself to the land;
Imagine you touch its raw edges
In all weather, time and again;

Imagine its colors; try
To imitate, day by day,
The morning's growth and the dusk,

The movement of all their creatures;
Surrender yourself, and be glad;
This is the law that endures.

6

The foothills of Tennessee,
The mountains of North Carolina,
Their rivers and villages

—Hiwassee and Cherokee,
The Cumberland, Pisgah and Nantahala,
Unaka and Unicoi—

Brindle and sing in your blood;
Their sounds are the sounds you hear,
Their shapes are the shapes you see

Regardless, whenever you concentrate
Upon the remembered earth
—All things that are are lights.

Jay Wright

The Charge

I

This is the morning.
There is a boy,

riding the shadow of a cradle,
clapping from room to room
as swift as the memory of him.
But it is no memory.
I did not come at this hour.
And if I had,
and if I were a memory,
would I be here now,
fully awake,
as sure of your memory
as of myself
who would be your memory?
These sounds, this image,
are not memory,
but the heart's throb past all defeats,
a livable assertion.
Now,
I hear you whistle through the house,
pushing wheels, igniting fires,
leaving no sound untried,
no room in which a young boy,
at sea in a phantom cradle,
could lurch and scream
and come to settle in the house.
You are so volubly alone,
that I turn,
reaching into the light for the boy
your father charged you to deliver.

II

We stand, and watch
my young wife's body rise and fall.
We wait to release ourselves
with the cry that makes the moon sway.
Soon,

there will be dancing,
a slow retreat to the water,
where women will hold the boy
plucked from the weeds,
a manchild, discovered,
waiting.
That is the memory
that will begin it,
an unconscious possession
of what coming like rain,
and the image of rain, can mean.

III

Now, father,
I am yours again,
and you belong to him
and the father who charged you.
But it isn't true yet.
I have only been dreaming,
and caught in the dream
of bringing him here,
where what is given
is only a memory,
and still no memory,
where death is all I have
to offer him,
though I go on living,
drawing closer, as I age, to you.
Even in this dream,
I call you to come to him.
Even though this is no more than a dream,
I call you to argue him
into existence.
No,
no word is enough.

210

Even the image will not come again,
unless I give it my assent.

IV

Careful in everything,
we have prepared a place,
just at that spot
where the sun forever enters this circle.
Fathers and sons sit,
making the noise of fathers,
waiting for the cut
into the life of my son,
waiting for my modest life
to be as whole as theirs.
All things here move
with that global rhythm.
All memories come
after the heat of it.
We are petals,
closed at evening,
opening at the first touch.
We are gathered to watch
the shaping of another miracle.
We are gathered in the miracle
of our own memories.
Unhappy sun,
even you cannot light everything.

V

This is the morning
when I am fully awake
to your sadness.
Now, father,
I am more than yours,
and lead you past the tricks

of our memory,
into this moment
as real as memory.
This is the moment
when all our unwelcome deaths
charge us to be free.
And my late son,
no savior,
rises still to fill
our vacant eyes.

C.K. Williams

Waking Jed

Deep asleep, perfect immobility, no apparent evidence of consciousness or of dream.

Elbow cocked, fist on pillow lightly curled to the tension of the partially relaxing sinew.

Head angled off, just so: the jaw's projection exaggerated slightly, almost to prognathous: why?

The features express nothing whatsoever and seem to call up no response in me.

Though I say nothing, don't move, gradually, far down within, he, or rather not *he* yet,

something, a presence, an element of being, becomes aware of me: there begins a subtle,

very gentle alteration in the structure of the face, or maybe less than that, more elusive,

as though the soft distortions of sleep-warmth radiating from his face and flesh,

those essentially unreal mirages in the air between us, were
modifying, dissipating.
The face is now more his, Jed's—its participation in the
almost Romanesque generality
I wouldn't a moment ago have been quite able to specify,
not having its contrary, diminishes.
Particularly on the cheekbones and chin, the skin is thin-
ning, growing denser, harder,
the molecules on the points of bone coming to attention,
the eyelids finer, brighter, foil-like:
capillaries, veins; though nothing moves, there are goings
to and fro behind now.
One hand opens, closes down more tightly, the arm extends
suddenly full length,
jerks once at the end, again, holds: there's a more pro-
nounced elongation of the skull—
the infant pudginess, whatever atavism it represented, or
reversion, has been called back.
Now I sense, although I can't say how, his awareness of me:
I can feel him begin to *think,*
I even know that he's thinking—or thinking in a dream
perhaps—of me, watching him here.
Now I'm aware—again, with no notion how, nothing indi-
cates it—that if there was a dream,
it's gone, and, yes, his eyes abruptly open although his gaze,
straight before him,
seems not to register just yet, the mental operations still
independent of his vision.
I say his name, the way we do it, softly, calling one another
from a cove or cave,
as though something else were there with us, not to be
disturbed, to be crept along beside.
The lids come down again, he yawns, widely, very con-
sciously manifesting intentionality.
Great, if rudimentary pleasure now: a sort of primitive,
peculiarly mammalian luxury—

to know, to know wonderfully that lying here, warm, pro-
    tected, eyes closed, one can,
for a moment anyway, a precious instant, put off the lower
    specie onsets, duties, debts.
Sleeker, somehow, slyer, more aggressive now, he is sud-
    denly more awake, all awake,
already plotting, scheming, fending off: nothing said but
    there is mild rebellion, conflict:
I insist, he resists, and then, with abrupt, wriggling grace,
    he otters down from sight,
just his brow and crown, his shining rumpled hair, left
    ineptly showing from the sheet.
Which I pull back to find him in what he must believe a
    parody of sleep, himself asleep:
fetal, rigid, his arms clamped to his sides, eyes screwed shut,
    mouth clenched, grinning.

Marvin Bell

Letting in Cold

Who killed Christ?—my favorite subject.
You misunderstood my love for Russia,
going so far you changed love into hate,
which was not my intention. You know,
in your time you changed life into death,
what-is to what-is-not, schooling to recess.
The enigmatic lesson in geography! that

wasn't the teacher's way of instructing
but only my way of trying propriety.
The proper study of man is where he came from!

You came from Russia—under the hayloads,
bareback to Poland, steerage to America.
The tip of the whip the teacher withdraws
comes all the way from a bitter Europe.

Today, here, the first new snow
bothers the softness in people, and they are kind.
In four months, the world will seem harsh
as ever, a localness, a locking-out that continues,
and we will stand corrected, half-dead and
corrected. No one approaches the father's thoughts
where he stands, at the back door, letting in cold.

Marvin Bell

Treetops

My father moves through the South hunting duck.
It is warm, he has appeared
like a ship, surfacing, where he floats, face up,
through the ducklands. Over the tops
of trees duck will come, and he strains
not to miss seeing the first of each flock,
although it will be impossible to shoot one
from such an angle, face up like that
in a floating coffin where the lid obstructs
half a whole view, if he has a gun.
Afterlives are full of such hardships.

One meets, for example, in one's sinlessness,
high water and our faithlessness,
so the dead wonder if they are imagined
but they are not quite.

How could they know we know
when the earth shifts deceptively
to set forth ancestors to such pursuits?
My father will be asking, Is this fitting?
And I think so—I, who, with the others,
coming on the afterlife after the fact
in a dream, in a probable volume, in a
probable volume of dreams, think so.

Marvin Bell

To an Adolescent Weeping Willow

I don't know what you think you're doing,
sweeping the ground. You
do it so easily, backhanded, forehanded.
You hardly bend. Really, you sway.
What can it mean
when a thing is so easy?

I threw dirt on my father's floor.
Not dirt, but a chopped green
dirt which picked up dirt.

I pushed the pushbroom.
I oiled the wooden floor of the store.

He bent over and lifted the coal
into the coalstove. With the back of the shovel
he came down on the rat just topping the bin
and into the fire.

What do you think? —Did he sway?
Did he kiss a rock for luck?
Did he soak up water
and climb into light and turn and turn?

Did he weep and weep in the yard?

Yes, I think he did. Yes,
now I think he did.

So, Willow, you come sweep my floor.
I have no store.
I have a yard. A big yard.

I have a song to weep.
I have a cry.

You who rose up from the dirt,
because I put you there
and like to walk my head in under
your earliest feathery branches—
what can it mean
when a thing is so easy?

It means you are a boy.

Jim Harrison

Suite to Fathers
for D.L.

I

I think that night's our balance,
our counterweight—a blind woman

we turn to for nothing but dark.
*
In Val-Mont I see a slab of parchment
a black quill pen in stone.
In a sculptor's garden
there was a head made from stone,
large as a room, the eyes neatly hooded
staring out with a crazed somnolence
fond of walled gardens.
*
The countesses arch like cats in chateaux.
They wake up as countesses and usually sleep with counts.
Nevertheless he writes them painful letters,
thinking of Eleanor of Aquitaine, Gaspara Stampa.
With Kappus he calls forth the stone in the rose.
*
In Egypt the dhows sweep the Nile
with ancient sails. I am in Egypt,
he thinks, this Baltic jew—it is hot,
how can I make bricks with no straw?
His own country rich with her food and slaughter,
fit only for sheep and generals.
*
He thinks of the coffin of the East,
of the tiers of dead in Venice,
those countless singulars.
At lunch, the baked apple too sweet with kirsch
becomes the tongues of convent girls at gossip,
under the drum and shadow of pigeons
the girl at promenade has almond in her hair.
*
From Duino, beneath the mist,
the green is so dark and green it cannot bear itself.
In the night, from black paper
I cut the silhouette of this exiled god,
finding him as the bones of a fish in stone.

218

II

In the cemetery the grass is pale,
fake green as if dumped from Easter baskets,
from overturned clay and the deeper marl
which sits in wet gray heaps by the creek.
There are no frogs, death drains there.
Landscape of glass, perhaps Christ
will quarry you after the worms.
The newspaper says caskets float in leaky vaults.
Above me, I feel paper birds.
The sun is a brass bell.
This is not earth I walk across
but the pages of some giant magazine.
*
Come song,
allow me some eloquence,
good people die.
*
The June after you died
I dove down into a lake,
the water turned to cold, then colder,
and ached against my ears.
I swam under a sunken log then paused,
letting my back rub against it,
like some huge fish with rib cage
and soft belly open to the bottom.
I saw the light shimmering far above
but did not want to rise.
*
It was so far up from the dark—
once it was night three days,
after that four, then six and over again.
The nest was torn from the tree,
the tree from the ground,
the ground itself sinking torn.

I envied the dead their sleep of rot.

I was a fable to myself,
a speech to become meat.

III

Once in Nevada I sat on a boulder at twilight—
I had no ride and wanted to avoid the snakes.
I watched the full moon rise a fleshy red
out of the mountains, out of a distant sandstorm.
I thought then if I might travel deep enough
I might embrace the dead as equals,
not in their separate stillnesses as dead, but in music
one with another's harmonies.
The moon became paler,
rising, floating upwards in her arc
and I with her, intermingled in her whiteness,
until at dawn again she bloodied
herself with earth.

*

In the beginning I trusted in spirits,
slight things, those of the dead in procession,
the household gods in mild delirium
with their sweet round music and modest feasts.
Now I listen only to that hard black core,
a ball harsh as coal, rending for light
far back in my own sour brain.

*

The tongue knots itself
a cramped fist of music,
the oracle a white-walled room of bone
which darkens now with a greater dark;
and the brain a glacier of blood,
inching forward, sliding, the bottom
silt covered but sweet,

becoming a river now
laving the skull with coolness—
the leaves on her surface
dipping against the bone.
*
Voyager, the self the voyage—
dark let me open your lids.
Night stares down with her great bruised eye.

Michael S. Harper

Nightmare Begins Responsibility

I place these numbed wrists to the pane
watching white uniforms whisk over
him in the tube-kept
prison
fear what they will do in experiment
watch my gloved stickshifting gasolined hands
breathe *boxcar-information-please* infirmary tubes
distrusting white-pink mending paperthin
silkened end hairs, distrusting tubes
shrunk in his *trunk-skincapped*
shaven head, in thighs
distrusting-white-hands-picking-baboon-light
on this son who will not make his second night
of this wardstrewn intensive airpocket
where his father's asthmatic
hymns of *night-train,* train done gone
his mother can only know that he has flown
up into essential calm unseen corridor

going boxscarred home, *mamaborn, sweetsonchild*
gonedowntown into *researchtestingwarehousebatteryacid*
mama-son-done-gone/me telling her 'nother
train tonight, no music, no breathstroked
heartbeat in my infinite distrust of them:

and of my distrusting self
white-doctor-who-breathed-for-him-all-night
say it for two sons gone,
say nightmare, say it loud
panebreaking heartmadness:
nightmare begins responsibility.

Michael S. Harper

We Assume: On the Death of Our Son, Reuben Masai Harper

We assume
that in 28 hours,
lived in a collapsible isolette,
you learned to accept pure oxygen
as the natural sky;
the scant shallow breaths
that filled those hours
cannot, did not make you fly—
but dreams were there
like crooked palmprints on
the twin-thick windows of the nursery—
in the glands of your mother.

We assume
the sterile hands
drank chemicals in and out
from lungs opaque with mucus,
pumped your stomach,
eeked the bicarbonate in
crooked, green-winged veins,
out in a plastic mask;

A woman who'd lost her first son
consoled us with an angel gone ahead
to pray for our family—
gone into that sky
seeking oxygen,
gone into autopsy,

a fine brown powdered sugar,
a disposable cremation:

We assume
you did not know we loved you.

Charles Simic

George Simic

1

Captain,
what are you doing
with that cane?
There are no dogs here anymore.
The blind-alley has eyes now.

Did you carve it from our threshold
while the new owners slept?
You are its father too;
it skips ahead of you, chattering.
When a hump grew on your back,
a shadow came to be its sister.

2

Like a fisherman, alone
on a quiet autumn lake:
the smoke of your cigar—
has the thought bitten?
I give you back the hair I stole
from your sleeping ear.
It has grown, hollow.
Blow on it as you would
on a layer of fine dust,
whistle back our old life.

3

That in you which belongs
to your mother playing the accordion,
that in me which belongs
to a glass of wine raised in your hand...
I hired my voice
to its sheen.
No one dies there,
no one walks alone.
The bullet they fire is white,
so is our wound.

4

If you sing now,
the table will lift itself.

If you sing now,
a beautiful woman will bare her breast.
Such clarity, it is a lens
to see far with eyes shut:
three meadows and no shadow to be found,
three meadows only one barren pear tree
like a mourner
left at the gravesite.

5

Who did we hire out to?
Who sent us early one morning,
hunger's own hirelings,
for that kettle of lentils
simmering on the stove,
for the rooster crowing at the kitchen window?
A story of footprints
that came to an end abruptly:
a place without landmarks,
a place for great dreamers.

6

Now I want to see the cleft-
footed one, the one with pig's ears,
the son of a bitch who washes
his ass in our milk, who anoints us
in his bile on the sly,
who on all evidence doesn't exist.
In the name of our sacred right
to our own madness, in the name
of our brotherhood of fear,
I want to spit over my shoulder.

7

We spoke of winters,
snowbound travellers.
We spoke of fires
neither dead nor alive.
Dawn came, dawn of laborers:
the coffee's steam was visible.
You've been gone long, old man.
With whom do you cut cards,
dog-eared, greasy cards,
black on both sides?

Frank Bidart

Golden State

I

To see my father
lying in pink velvet, a rosary
twined around his hands, rouged,
lipsticked, his skin marble...

My mother said, "He looks the way he did
thirty years ago, the day we got married,—
I'm *glad* I went;
I was afraid: now I can remember him
like that..."

Ruth, your last girlfriend, who wouldn't sleep with you
or marry, because you wanted her

to pay half the expenses, and "His drinking
almost drove me crazy—"
                              Ruth once saw you
staring into a mirror,
in your ubiquitous kerchief and cowboy hat,
say:
      "Why can't I look like a cowboy?"

You left a bag of money; and were
the unhappiest man
I have ever known well.

                    II

It's in many ways
a relief to have you dead.
                              I have more money.
Bakersfield is easier: life isn't so nude,
now that I no longer have to
face you each evening: mother is progressing
beautifully in therapy, I can almost convince myself
a good analyst would have saved you:

for I *need* to believe, as
always, that your pervasive sense of disappointment

proceeded from
trivial desires: but I fear
that beneath the wish to be a movie star,
cowboy, empire builder, all those
cheap desires, lay
radical disaffection
                    from the very possibilities
of human life...

Your wishes were too simple:
                    or too complex.

III

I find it difficult to imagine you
in bed, making love to a woman...

By common consensus, you were a *good* lover:
and yet,
mother once said: "Marriage would be better
if it weren't mixed up with sex..."

Just after the divorce,—when I was
about five,—I slept all night with you

in a motel, and again and again
you begged me
to beg her to come back...

I said nothing; but she went back
several times, again and again
you would go on a binge, there would be
another woman,
mother would leave...

You always said,
"Your mother is the only woman I've ever loved."

IV

Oh Shank, don't turn into the lies
of mere, neat poetry...

I've been reading Jung, and he says that we can
never get to the bottom
of what is, or was...

But *why* things were as they were
obsesses; I know that you
the necessity to contend with you
your *helplessness*

before yourself,
                    —has been at the center
of how I think my life . . .

                              And yet your voice, raw,
demanding, dissatisfied,
saying over the telephone:

        "How are all those bastards at Harvard?"

remains, challenging: beyond all the
patterns and paradigms
                        I use to silence and stop it.

                    V

I dreamed I *had* my wish:
                        —I seemed to see
the conditions of my life, upon
a luminous stage: how I could change,
how I could not: the root of necessity,
and choice.
            The stage was labelled
"Insight."
            The actors there
had no faces, I cannot remember
the patterns of their actions, but
simply by watching,

I knew that beneath my feet
the fixed stars
governing my life

had begun to fall, and melt . . .
                        —Then your face appeared,

laughing at the simplicity of my wish.

VI

Almost every day
I take out the letter you wrote me in Paris.
. . . Why?

It was written
the year before you married Shirley; Myrtle,
your girlfriend, was an ally of mine
because she "took care of you,"
but you always
made it clear
she was too dumpy and crude to marry . . .

In some ways "elegant,"
with a pencil-thin, neatly clipped moustache,
chiselled, Roman nose, you were
a millionaire
and always pretended
you couldn't afford to go to Europe . . .

When I was a child,
you didn't seem to care if I existed.

Bakersfield, Calif
July 9, 1961

Dear Pinon.

Sorry I haven't wrote to you sooner but glad to hear
that you are well and enjoying *Paris*.

I got your fathers day wire in the hospital where I put
in about twelve days but I am very well now. I quit the
ciggaretts but went through ten days of hell quitting and
my back had been giving me hell.

It had been very hot here but the last few days has
been very nice. Emily just got out of the hospital yesterday.
She had her feet worked on. I guess she will tell you about
it. Glad to hear you are learning some French.

230

We are just about through with potatoes. Crop was very good but no price at all whitch made it a poor year. Cattle are cheap too. It look like a bad year for all farmer's.

I don't know anything else to tell you. Take care of your self and enjoy it. Maybe you will never have another chance for another trip. I don't think I'll ever get the chance to go, so if you run into a extra special gal between 28 & 35 send her over here to me as all I know over here don't amount to mutch. Well I guess I'll close now as I am going over to see Emily.

Hoping to hear from you right away.

This address is 4019 Eton St. be sure and get it straight. Myrtle would like to know how much that watch amounts to. Let us know

Will close now and write soon.

Love 'Shank'

P.S. Excuse this writing as its about 30 years since I wrote a letter.

VII

How can I say this?
                    I think my psychiatrist
likes me: he knows
the most terrible things I've done, every stupidity,
inadequacy, awkwardness,
ignorance, the mad girl I screwed
because she once again and again
teased and rejected me, and whose psychic incompetence
I grimly greeted as an occasion for revenge;
he greets my voice

with an interest, and regard, and affection,
which seem to signal I'm worth love;

—you finally

forgave me for being your son, and in the nasty
shambles of your life, in which you had less and less
occasion for pride, you were proud
of me, the first Bidart
who ever got a B.A.; Harvard, despite
your distrust, was the crown;—but the way
you eyed me:
                    the *bewilderment,* unease:
the somehow always
tentative, suspended judgment...

—however *much* you tried (and, clearly,
you *did* try)
                    you could not remake your
taste, and like me: could not remake
yourself, to give me

the grace
needed to look in a mirror, as I often can
now, with some equanimity...

VIII

When did I begin to substitute
insight, for prayer?...

                    —You believed in neither:
but said, "My life is over,"
after you had married Shirley,
twenty-five years younger, with three
small children, the youngest
six months old; she was unfaithful
within two months, the marriage was simply
annulled...
                    A diabetic, you didn't
take your insulin when you drank, and
almost managed to die

many times...
                    You punished Ruth
when she went to Los Angeles for a weekend, by
beginning to drink; she would return home
either to find you in the hospital,
or in a coma on the floor...

                              The exacerbation

of this seeming *necessity*
for connection—;
                    you and mother taught me
there's little that's redemptive or useful
in natural affections...

I must *unlearn;* I must believe
you were merely a man—
with a character, and a past—;
                              you wore them,
                              unexamined,

like a nimbus of
furies

round your
greying, awesome head...

                              IX

What should I have done? In 1963,
you wanted to borrow ten thousand dollars
from me, so that we could buy cattle
together, under the name "Bidart and Son,"—
most of your money was tied up
in the increasingly noxious "Bidart Brothers,"
run by your brother, Johnny...

I said no,—
that I wanted to use the money

for graduate school; but I thought
if you went on a binge, and as had happened
before, simply threw it away...

The Bidarts agreed
you were *not* to be trusted; you accepted
my answer, with an air
of inevitability I was shocked at...

I didn't *want* to see your self-disgust;
—somehow, your self-congratulation
had eroded more deeply, much
more deeply, than even I had wished,—

but for *years,* how I had wished!...

I have a friend who says
that he has never felt a conflict
between something deeply wished or desired,
and what he thought was "moral"...

Father, such innocence
surely is a kind of *Eden*—; but,
somehow, I can't regret that we
are banished from that company—;
in the awareness, the
history of our contradictions and violence,
insofar as I am "moral" at all,
is the beginning of my moral being.

X

When I began this poem,
                              to see myself
as a piece of history, having a past
which shapes, and informs, and thus inevitably
limits—
              at first this seemed sufficient, the beginning of

freedom...
                The way to approach freedom
was to acknowledge necessity:—
I sensed I had to become not merely
a speaker, the "eye," but a character...

And you had to become a character: with a past,
with a set of internal contradictions and necessities
which if I could *once* define, would at least
begin to release us from each other...

But, of course, no such knowledge is possible;—
as I touch your photographs, they stare back at me
with the dazzling, impenetrable, glitter of mere life...

You stand smiling, at the end of the twenties,
in a suit, and hat,
cane and spats, with a collie at your feet,
happy to be handsome, dashing, elegant:—

and though I cannot connect this image

with the end of your life, with the defensive
gnarled would-be cowboy,—
you seem happy at that fact, happy
to be surprising; unknowable; unpossessable...

You say it's what you always understood by freedom.
                                            1968–69

Stanley Plumly

Now That My Father Lies Down Beside Me

We lie in that other darkness, ourselves.
There is less than the width of my left hand

between us. I can barely breathe,
but the light breathes easily,
wind on water across our two still bodies.

I cannot even turn to see him.
I would not touch him. Nor would I lift
my arm into the crescent of a moon.
(There is no star in the sky of this room,
only the light fashioning fish along the walls.
They swim and swallow one another.)

I dream we lie under water,
caught in our own sure drift.
A window, white shadow, trembles over us.
Light breaks into a moving circle.
He would not speak and I would not touch him.

It is an ocean under here.
Whatever two we were, we become
one falling body, one breath. Night lies down
at the sleeping center—no fish, no shadow,
no single, turning light. And I would not touch him
who lies deeper in the drifting dark than life.

Stanley Plumly

Out-of-the-Body Travel

1

And then he would lift this finest
of furniture to his big left shoulder

and tuck it in and draw the bow
so carefully as to make the music

almost visible on the air. And play
and play until a whole roomful of the sad
relatives mourned. They knew this was
drawing of blood, threading and rethreading

the needle. They saw even in my father's
face how well he understood the pain
he put them to—his raw, red cheek
pressed against the cheek of the wood...

2

And in one stroke he brings the hammer
down, like mercy, so that the young bull's
legs suddenly fly out from under it...
While in the dream he is the good angel

in Chagall, the great ghost of his body
like light over the town. The violin
sustains him. It is pain remembered.
Either way, I know if I wake up cold,

and go out into the clear spring night,
still dark and precise with stars,
I will feel the wind coming down hard
like his hand, in fever, on my forehead.

Stanley Plumly

After Grief

When you woke up among them,
when you rose,
when you got up and they asked you
what you were—*is it named?*—
and you in your new clothes
and face and body lined dry with newspaper,

when you climbed out of the coffin
and began to walk,
alive (*like a rainbow* one of them said),
without a word, in this place of skull and femur,
stone and the sounds of water, when you walked up
to the one talking, his face a face
of the moon, and started to speak, he said

no need, I know who you are.

All this recorded in the first book, The Dream,
The Book of the Dead, in the blessing
of the death of each day.

And tonight, bedded down,
the mind adrift, the body just a few feet
from the earth, it is written:

there is the river,
go wash yourself.
And you asked
what is this place? And the one
without a face answered
look around you, this is where you are.

I remember how even near the end
you would go out to your garden
just before dark, in the blue air,
and brood over the failures

of corn and cabbage
or the crooked row
but meaning the day had once more
failed for you.

I watched you as any son watches his father,
like prophecy.

And in my mind I counted the thousand
things to say.

And tonight, again, it is written
that the one talking said
Father, forgive everything.
leave these clothes, this body,
they are nothing.
lie down in the water.
be whole.

And having done so, you rose
among them, who are called The Bones,
without flesh or face.

All this recorded in the dream unending.

The first death was the death of the father.
And whosoever be reborn in sons
so shall they be also reborn.

In The Book of the Dead are names
the weight of the continents.
At each rising of the waters
shall the earth be washed:

this is the dream that holds the planet
in place.

And you, my anonymous father,
be with me when I wake.

Paul Mariani

A Walk in Early March
For Mark

Of the manner in which he moves
over the yellow stubble furrows
of early March with his mongrel
dog as he has for years now. Of
the dog's limping gait, rear legs
arthritic, doing fewer elliptical
sorties this year out from his
master and back.
                Of that straight
back, strong as a young ash tree,
of that quiet, self-assured gait,
the blond hair along the tanned arms,
of the thick blond hair of that head,
hair I have cut myself now
for fourteen years, of the reassuring
voice, the gaiety of those
gray blue eyes, his mother's.
Bone of our bone. A son. The fact
the mystery we call fatherhood. Of
the cry, the utterance as I break
the stillness with words, then return
to the depths of that stillness.
The counter-response, his head half
turning in acknowledgment. The fact
of chill air whisked suddenly across
my chest but with the promise of warmth
in it, the coarse sand and large stones
dragged up by the thick ice slabs
on the river and left there when the ice
melted under last month's early rains.
The ground with hints of green here

and there—wildcarrot—spongy, yielding
to our weight.

        Of the manner in which,
quietly, he stops and turns to his right,
peering into the swift flowing Sawmill
at something golden he invites me
to share. A smooth stone? a rusting beercan?
his dog sensing his chance bringing his head
up against his leg, nudging his hand
to be stroked. And he is.
        Of the manner too
in which, by the fact of his presence,
he has half taught his father the hard
lessons of courtesy, of keeping the voice
down, lessons other than those the father
learned for himself as a boy on the City's
East Side, how for example to rush out
between cars and huddle in the dark doorways
of tenements when the bullies had spied him,
how to pull away from the tall lonely
strangers who tried to press candy bars
and something more on him, how to leap
from tenement to dizzy tenement five stories
off the ground, the face hugging the pitch
of the roof warmed with the spring sun.

Of the lesson of learning to listen
for the faint, distinct cry
of the whippoorwill, of hearing the thin
bellicosity of the ancient donkey
who still inhabits this fallow pasture, of
catching the faint glimmer of gold
from the old stone caught in the icecold
bracing stream to be pored over,
delighted in, left miraculously intact.

James Reiss

The Green Tree

Ever since my daughters started to walk
I have had increasing difficulty with my eyes.
I remember the day Wendy took her first steps, when
she said "bamboo" and waddled over to pat the rusty bumper

of a truck, I could barely make out the writing
scrawled in dirt on the trailer and had trouble focusing
as she stepped into its shadow.
The morning in Maine when she raced down the beach

and splashed into the ocean before I could reach her,
I actually mistook her for another little girl in pink
whom—I am sorry to say—I began leading slowly out of the
        water.
Then there is Jill: when she first walked I remember

looking at her and thinking, "I am a camera fading back, back
Years later when she would go rollerskating with Wendy
my eyes were so bad I could no longer tell
where the sidewalks left off and my daughters began.

By now everything has faded into fine print. I
have been to a doctor who says he is also troubled,
but has sons. My only son died one day after
birth, weighing two pounds. His name was

Jeffrey, but I have always preferred to call him "Under-the-
        Earth"
or, especially on rainy days, "Under-the-Sod." In fact,
sometimes I catch myself repeating these words: "My only son
Under-the-Sod, is playing over there by the green tree."

Paul Zweig

Father

I

I want to be near this mild unforgiving man,
Who comes from my hands and voice,
And is the nervous laughter
I hear before my throat expels it.

For years he slept days, worked nights,
Rode a bicycle when only boys did.
I remember his walks on the beach,
His face, so stubborn, so quiet, it frightened me,
Yet may only have been shy.

I imagine him hugging some gift
Along the Brooklyn streets when he was a boy,
Working at his father's laundry.
He preserved it in his mind,
A timeless falling world where he still lives.
And the gift was for me:
An amazed distance only acrobats could leap.

II

Father, there are things I never asked you,
Now the answers seem trivial.
Yet, for all your angry quiet, your shy muscular body,
What did you save by living less?
Except maybe on those solitary walks,
Hearing the rustle of your beloved ocean
Which never cried for an answer,
Or beat at you with insatiate fists.

III

I think of your swallowed angers,
The pain on your face when I twisted grammar.

All your life you wrestled with fears that would not become ange
Inside your crabbed masculinity, was a motherly sweetness
You could let out only when you were alone,
With the damp sand under your feet, the foaming waves beside
With an artistry I still marvel at,
You remade yourself in that lonely space,
As you have remade yourself in me.

James Tate

The Lost Pilot
for my father, 1922–1944

Your face did not rot
like the others—the co-pilot,
for example, I saw him

yesterday. His face is corn-
mush: his wife and daughter,
the poor ignorant people, stare

as if he will compose soon.
He was more wronged than Job.
But your face did not rot

like the others—it grew dark,
and hard like ebony;
the features progressed in their

distinction. If I could cajole
you to come back for an evening,
down from your compulsive

244

orbiting, I would touch you,
read your face as Dallas,
your hoodlum gunner, now,

with the blistered eyes, reads
his braille editions. I would
touch your face as a disinterested

scholar touches an original page.
However frightening, I would
discover you, and I would not

turn you in; I would not make
you face your wife, or Dallas,
or the co-pilot, Jim. You

could return to your crazy
orbiting, and I would not try
to fully understand what

it means to you. All I know
is this: when I see you,
as I have seen you at least

once every year of my life,
spin across the wilds of the sky
like a tiny, African god,

I feel dead. I feel as if I were
the residue of a stranger's life,
that I should pursue you.

My head cocked toward the sky,
I cannot get off the ground,
and, you, passing over again,

fast, perfect, and unwilling
to tell me that you are doing
well, or that it was mistake

that placed you in that world,
and me in this; or that misfortune
placed these worlds in us.

_____

Dave Smith

The Pornography Box

At eighteen, the U.S. Navy eye chart
memorized, reciting what was unseen,
my father enlisted for the duration.
At nineteen he caught a casual wave
wrong off Norfolk, our home, called
Hell by sailors. The landing craft
cast him loose and burst his knee.
He lived, and wore his rigid brace
without complaint, and never in his
life showed anyone his Purple Heart.
I stumbled into that brace and more
when I climbed to our sealed attic
the year a drunk blindsided him
to death in a ditch, and me to worse.

Today I watch my ten-year-old son race
over the slick pages of _Playboy,_
ashamed I brought it home, imagining
his unasked questions have answers.
I remember the chairs I stacked
and climbed, the brace I put on
to see how it felt and, buried
deep in his sea chest, the livid
shapes shoved so far in a slit

of darkness a man could reach them
only hunched, on all fours. I clawed
through families of discharged clothes,
ornaments for Christmas, to feel
the spooky silk of webs slickly
part on my face where blood rushed.

Trussed on their wide bed, my mother lay
surviving wreckage, stitched back
beyond the secrets I knew he kept.
I shimmied through a dark hole
in the ceiling and listened to pine
rake the roof like a man's shuffle.
But he was dead and the box unlocked.
His flashlight pulsed through my body,
each glossy pose burning my eyes
that knew only air-brush innocence.
Sex rose in me like a first beard.
A woman with painted nails peeled
a foreskin, another held a man
kingly rigid at her tongue's tip.
I could not catch my breath.

I blinked at one spread on a table covered
by lace grandmotherly clean and white.
Here might have been service for tea,
dainty cups, bread, a butter dish,
except she was in their place, clearly
young in middy suit. Behind her a vase
of daisies loomed, the parlor wall
held *Home, Sweet Home* in needlepoint,
and curtains were luminous at a window.
I remember the eyes, direct and flat,
as if she had died. Girlish stockings
knuckled at her knees, her plain skirt
neatly rolled. The man, in Victorian
suit, cradled her calves in furred hands,

and looked at the window, placid as
a navigator. He cut her like a knife.

After school, at night, weekend afternoons,
I raced to see them do it, legs cramped
in that freezing slot of darkness, gone
wobbly as a sailor into the country.
I came and went in the black tube,
ashamed, rooting like a hog to see.
In one sequence a black man held a pool
cue to a white woman, a black woman
held in both hands white and black balls.
The uniforms of sailors were scattered,
wadded everywhere I looked. I smelled
the mothballs from my father's chest
when late at night I woke to vomit
and stare at a clock's one-eyed glow.

How long does it go on, the throbbing dream,
waking obsessed with a hole in the air?
In Norfolk, from loaded cars, we spilled
at sailors passing alleys, asking where
we'd find some girls, beer, a good time.
All answers were sucker-punched. *Bye-bye,
Seafood,* we screamed, then headed down
toward the Gaiety Theater and whores
bright as moths. We spit at mothers who
yelled *Fuck you, kid!* They never would.
The secrets of our fathers, we cruised
the hopeless streets blank as razors,
remembering nothing but naked images
whose neon flared like pus. Seeing now
my son bent to see I imagine at last
my father climbing before me in blackness,
with the tiny light a man carries, bent
on pained knees where I will kneel also

at nameless images we each live to love
and fear. One is a young Spanish dancer
whose crinolines flare out around her
hidden rose. Another cooks in high heels.
Among these are angels, blonde sisters,
classmates suddenly gone from our towns,
one on a patio reclined, her long leg
crooked in invitation. She does not hide
the shorter leg. Each grins and burns
into our memory, speaking in shy whispers,
who are born to teach us violations.
At eighteen what fathers teach is wrong,
for the world is wrong, and only women
know why, their eyes dark and flat.

It isn't eyes that sons remember, blinded
by what never lies or leaves, but
sun's glint on that raw breast, that
thigh where face should not be but is,
and is the curve of the world's flesh
radiant in its rottenness, the secret
that leaves, finally apart and other,
all who walk on the earth. In memory
I see how each breast, each leg, each
face hissed our shame. By accident
I became the boy-father of the house,
owner of obscenities and a family
of creeps who fingered me as one.
What else is the world but a box,
false-bottomed, where the ugly truths
wait sailing in the skins of ancestors?

Escaping them at last I left for college.
But first climbed to what he left me,
carted that box and brace to grave,
and spilled those mild faces down

under the looming Baptist spire.
I spread gasoline where he lay, then
with his Navy Zippo snapped it off.
Quick bodies coiled and flamed, ash
flecks disappearing in sun forever.
I gouged the remains in a trench
of churchly dirt, tried once to spit,
then turned in the dark to catch a bus.
His pea-coat was black as the sea
at midnight but I took it and wore it,
sweating against the cold to come.

Women smiled at me as if I'd been flush
with cash from months at sea. *Welcome,
Swabby,* one said, *You can sit here.*
I was free, I thought, discharged from
Hell into the world that, for Christ's
sake, waited. I left home in a wink.
And would not go back at Christmas,
being after all busy, being holed up
with the nameless girl, the long blade
of her body even now slicing memory,
that darling who took my coat. But
by Easter was ready, went. House sold,
mother gone, maybe married, maybe Florida,
they said. I wandered in a cold sea-wind,
almost on shore leave, until I came
cast up where my father lay. Posters

of the nailed Jesus littered the grass,
announcing our inexplicable life. I saw
the crones kneeled there in sunbursts,
faceless, soft, as if to serve the sun
dying in the background. I shivered,
then rose up, hearing traffic hiss,
and walked until I found the old road.

I wished I had our goddamn stolen coat.
Boys yelled at me, but no one stopped.
Freed, I was myself. Who understands?
I walked hours in hard places, into night,
my first beard tingling, dreaming what
fathers know. I came to a seedy house.
Among sailors I, a man, heard the siren
call us forward to sit with the darkness
under reels of lighted, loving women
in the theater called Art's House.
At love's edge, braced, we were nineteen.

So we went in.

Daniel Halpern

The Summer Rentals
(For My Father)

Today we went to see the summer rentals
that belong to Mrs. Marian Forster.
Her house, up the road from the Camden marina,
was off to the left, placed on the bay
across from the Curtis Island lighthouse.

She was a talker, with a quick, momentary smile—
you would have likened it to a jab,
but would have liked her handsome good looks.
I thought of you because she had just married
a man she knew in Los Angeles thirty years ago

who was built like you, tall and thin, elegant
in his dark suit and tie. A European with your face,

had you lived long enough, and your good humor
that lived in the eyes. His name was Karl.
Over proper drinks we talked summer rentals

with Mrs. Forster, or Mrs. Someone Else now—
we weren't given Karl's last name.
It was clear from the way he watched her
he was in love for the first time,
or still in love with his first love.

Talking to him was like talking to you.
Although I don't think we spoke of anything
in particular, it was like the talk we had
tossing a ball back and forth outside our house,
or walking down Van Nuys Boulevard.

Mrs. Forster liked us—we were "an interesting couple."
She took Jeanne's face in her hands
and asked me, "Is this a summer thing?"
Mrs. Forster, working the world of possibility,
never lost the spirit of romance.

She showed us, with delicate speed, "the small house,"
in which we could hear the sounds of the bay—
but not as well as in her house, she explained.
The stove in our kitchen had only four burners
and used electric heat, on which she refused to cook,

hers being a Garland with six gas burners
and a salamander, suitable for her style of living.
She told us the guests who lived on her property
had keys to every door, but as we grew silent,
followed with a confirmation that she of all people

believed in the importance of privacy.
I wonder what you would have thought.
Certainly you would have voted against renting,
in spite of being charmed by Mrs. Forster
and her property's flawless situation on the water.

We returned to her house and the women wandered off
to look at other rooms, pieces of furniture,
photographs of the second wedding and of her first husband,
who remained one rarely referred to in that house.
Karl and I talked a bit about his work in California,

his new life with Mrs. Forster, and he even explained
that when Mr. Forster died he had arrived to take her
"out of the woods." I knew he was Swedish
by the quick intake of breath that occurred when I said
something he agreed with. His sidelong glance and smile

presented the one context we could share.
It seemed to me, as we talked, that he knew
I was talking to you.
It was his eyes that allowed me to imagine asking
the two or three things I've wanted to ask you.

For some reason, as we left, knowing it would be impossible to return,
I rememberd the first room I rented, against your better judgment,
as well as the room where I last saw you. I shook Karl's hand.
It was large and dry and surprisingly strong. As strong,
I returned the handshake you taught me as a boy.

Ira Sadoff

My Father's Leaving

When I came back, he was gone.
My mother was in the bathroom
crying, my sister in her crib
restless but asleep. The sun
was shining in the bay window,

the grass had just been cut.
No one mentioned the other woman,
nights he spent in that stranger's house.

I sat at my desk and wrote him a note.
When my mother saw his name on the sheet
of paper, she asked me to leave the house.
When she spoke, her voice was like a whisper
to someone else, her hand a weight
on my arm I could not feel.

In the evening, though, I opened the door
and saw a thousand houses just like ours.
I thought I was the one who was leaving,
and behind me I heard my mother's voice
asking me to stay. But I was thirteen
and wishing I were a man I listened
to no one, and no words from a woman
I loved were strong enough to make me stop.

Philip Schultz

For My Father
Samuel Schultz, 1903–1963

Spring we went into the heat of lilacs
& his black eyes got big as onions & his fat lower lip
hung like a bumper & he'd rub his chin's hard fur on my ch
& tell stories: he first saw America from his father's arms
& his father said here he could have anything if he wanted it
with all his life & he boiled soap in his back yard & sold it
    door to door

& invented clothespins shaped like fingers & cigarette lighters
that played *Stars & Stripes* when the lid snapped open.

Mornings he lugged candy into factories
& his vending machines turned peanuts into pennies
my mother counted on the kitchen table & nights he came home
tripping on his laces & fell asleep over dinner & one night
he carried me outside & said only God knew what God had up
     His sleeve
& a man only knew what he wanted & he wanted a big white house
with a porch so high he could see all the way back to Russia
& the black moon turned on the axis of his eye & his breath
filled the red summer air with whisky of first light.

The morning his heart stopped I borrowed money to bury him
& his eyes still look at me out of mirrors & I hear him kicking
the coalburner to life & can taste the peanut salt on his hands
& his advice on lifting heavy boxes helps with the books I lug
     town to town
& I still count thunder's distance in heartbeats as he taught me
     & one day
I watched the sun's great rose open over the ocean as I swayed
     on the bow
of the Staten Island Ferry & I was his father's age when he
     arrived
with one borrowed suit & such appetite for invention & the bridges
were mountains & the buildings gold & the sky lifted backward
like a dancer & her red hair fanning the horizon & my eyes burn-
     ing
in a thousand windows & the whole Atlantic breaking at my feet.

Larry Levis

Blue Stones
—for my son, Nicholas

I suspect
They will slide me onto a cold bed,
A bed that has been brought in,
Out of the night
And past the fraying brick of the warehouse,
Where maybe a workman took an afternoon nap,
And woke staring up
At what sky he could see through one window.
But if he kept staring,
And thought that the bed took its gray color
From the sky, and kept watching that sky
Even after he had finished his cigarette,
He might learn
How things outlive us.
And maybe he would be reminded that the body, too,
Is only a thing, a joke it kept trying to tell us,
And now the moment for hearing it
Is past.
All I will have to decide, then,
Is how to behave during
Those last weeks, when the drawers
Of the dresser remain closed,
And the mirror is calm, and reflects nothing,
And outside, tangled
In the hard branches,
The moon appears.
I see how poor it is,
How it owns nothing.
I look at it a long time, until
I feel empty, as if I had travelled on foot
For three days, and become simple,
The way light was simple on the backs
Of horses as my father approached them,

Quietly, with a bridle.
My father thought dying
Was like standing trial for crimes
You could not remember.
Then someone really does throw
The first stone.
It is blue,
And seems to be made of the sky itself.
The breath goes out of you.
Tonight, the smoke holds still
Against the hills and trees outside this town,
And there is no hope
Of acquittal.

*

But *you?* Little believer, little
Straight, unbroken, and tireless thing.
Someday, when you are twenty-four and walking through
The streets of a foreign city, Stockholm,
Or Trieste,
Let me go with you a little way,
Let me be that stranger you won't notice,
And when you turn and enter a bar full of young men
And women, and your laughter rises,
Like the stones of a path up a mountain,
To say that no one has died,
I promise I will not follow.
I will cross at the corner in my gray sweater.
I will not have touched you,
As I did, for so many years,
On the hair and the left shoulder.
I will silence my hand that wanted to.
I will put it in my pocket, and let it clutch
The cold, blue stones they give you,
As a punishment,
After you have lived.

Larry Levis

*To a Wall of Flame in a Steel
Mill, Syracuse, New York, 1969*

Except under the cool shadows of pines,
The snow is already thawing
Along this road...
Such sun, and wind.
I think my father longed to disappear
While driving through this place once,
In 1957.
Beside him, my mother slept in a gray dress
While his thoughts moved like the shadow
Of a cloud over houses,
And he was seized, suddenly, by his own shyness,
By his desire to be grass,
And simplified.
Was it brought on
By the road, or the snow, or the sky
With nothing in it?
He kept sweating and wiping his face
Until it passed,
And I never knew.
But in the long journey away from my father,
I took only his silences, his indifference
To misfortune, rain, stones, music, and grief.
Now, I can sleep beside this road
If I have to,
Even while the stars pale and go out,
And it is day.
And if I can keep secrets for years,
The way a stone retains a warmth from the sun,
It is because men like us
Own nothing, really.
I remember, once,
In the steel mill where I worked,

Someone opened the door of the furnace
And I glanced in at the simple,
Quick and blank erasures the flames made of iron,
Of everything on earth.
It was reverence I felt then, and did not know why.
I do not know even now why my father
Lived out his one life
Farming two hundred acres of gray Málaga vines
And peach trees twisted
By winter. They lived, I think,
Because his hatred of them was entire,
And wordless.
I still think of him staring into this road
Twenty years ago,
While his hands gripped the wheel harder,
And his wish to be no one made his body tremble,
Like the touch
Of a woman he could not see,
Her fingers drifting up his spine in silence
Until his loneliness was perfect,
And she let him go—
Her laughter turning into these sheets of black
And glassy ice that dislodge themselves,
And ride slowly out,
Onto the thawing river.

Larry Levis

Winter Stars

My father once broke a man's hand
Over the exhaust pipe of a John Deere tractor. The man,

Ruben Vasquez, wanted to kill his own father
With a sharpened fruit knife, & he held
The curved tip of it, lightly, between his first
Two fingers, so it could slash
Horizontally, & with surprising grace,
Across a throat. It was like a glinting beak in a hand,
And for a moment, the light held still
On the vines. When it was over,
My father simply went in & ate lunch, & then, as always,
Lay alone in the dark, listening to music.
He never mentioned it.

I never understood how anyone could risk his life,
Then listen to Vivaldi.

Sometimes, I go out into this yard at night,
And stare through the wet branches of an oak
In winter, & realize I am looking at the stars
Again. A thin haze of them, shining
And persisting.

It used to make me feel lighter, looking up at them.
In California, that light was closer.
In a California no one will ever see again,
My father is beginning to die. Something
Inside him is slowly taking back
Every word it ever gave him.
Now, if we try to talk, I watch my father
Search for a lost syllable as if it might
Solve everything, & though he can't remember, now,
The word for it, he is ashamed. . . .
If you can think of the mind as a place continually
Visited, a whole city placed behind
The eyes, & shining, I can imagine, now, its end—
As when the lights go off, one by one,
In a hotel at night, until at last

All of the travelers will be asleep, or until
Even the thin glow from the lobby is a kind
Of sleep; & while the woman behind the desk
Is applying more lacquer to her nails,
You can almost believe that the elevator,
As it ascends, must open upon starlight.

I stand out on the street, & do not go in.
This was our agreement, at my birth.

And for years I believed
That what went unsaid between us became empty,
And pure, like starlight, & it persisted.
I got everything wrong.
I wound up believing in words the way a scientist
Believes in carbon, after death.

Tonight, I'm talking to you, father, although
It is quiet here in the midwest, where a small wind,
The size of a wrist, wakes the cold again—
Which may be all that's left of you & me.

When I left home at seventeen, I left for good.

That pale haze of stars goes on & on,
Like laughter that has found a final, silent shape
On a black sky. It means everything
It cannot say. Look, it's empty out there, & cold.
Cold enough to reconcile
Even a father, even a son.

Michael Ryan

This Is a Poem for the Dead

fathers: naked, you stand for their big faces,
mouths stuffed flat, eyes weighted, your miserable dick
sticking out like a nose. Dressed, you're more
of a mother making dinner: those old dirt bags,
the lungs, sway inside your chest like tits
in a housedress. Perhaps you're frying liver
which shrinks like your father getting older.
You still smell him breathing all over
your skin. He drank himself to death.

Now each woman you meet is a giant.
You'd crawl up their legs & never come down.
Even when you think you're big enough
to touch them, his voice flies from under
your throat & "I love you" comes out
a drunk whimper. All you can do
is breathe louder. You're speaking
to the back of your mouth. Finally,
you admit you know nothing
about sex & drown the urge slowly
like a fat bird in oil.

Still, those wings inside you.
At the hot stove all day you feel yourself
rising, the kids wrapping themselves
around your legs oh it's sexual
this nourishing food for the family
your father stumbling through the door
calling to you Honey I'm home.

Thomas Lux

This Is a Poem for the Fathers
(—*& for Michael Ryan*)

Pal, in the Pals of Death Club
we always ask each other: Do we die
like this or do we live

like this? Even novitiates
can answer: No!
We answer before we glance

at our deathwatches, gifts
from particular graduations,
without noticing our wrists,

like the necks of buzzards,
poking from our sleeves.
It's an easy question,

for us. It's easier than choosing
between whiplash and caress: No!:
we *live* like this: blue lights,

black marks that start low
on the fingernail then grow
away. Excellent!

The main idea is to keep our flesh
over our bones and to listen
occasionally to our bodies: when

the blood in our hands lies
down, we should lie down also.
Maybe an example will make it

clear: our fathers who are dead
and our fathers who are alive, are embracing.
Yours reaching out of the grave,

mine reaching...Look
at it this way: Nobody's happy. Nobody.
But that's not the point.

This is: the teasing haunt
of affirmation, the thermometers burning
in the mouth of the gone....

David St. John

Hush
For My Son

The way a tired Chippewa woman
Who's lost a child gathers up black feathers,
Black quills & leaves
That she wraps & swaddles in a little bale, a shag
Cocoon she carries with her & speaks to always
As if it were the child,
Until she knows the soul has grown fat & clever,
That the child can find its own way at last;
Well, I go everywhere
Picking the dust out of the dust, scraping the breezes
Up off the floor, & gather them into a doll
Of you, to touch at the nape of the neck, to slip
Under my shirt like a rag—the way
Another man's wallet rides above his heart. As you
Cry out, as if calling to a father you conjure
In the paling light, the voice rises, instead, in me.
Nothing stops it, the crying. Not the clove of moon,
Not the woman raking my back with her words. Our letters
Close. Sometimes, you ask

About the world; sometimes, I answer back. Nights
Return you to me for a while, as sleep returns sleep
To a landscape ravaged
& familiar. The dark watermark of your absence, a hush.

Bruce Smith

Window

There is a story so true, so becoming, so full of duty
and engraved love that it's glass—
a brittle crazy thing to see a father through.
It's like this: my father made a hole in the second story
chipping the brick the way a wasp hits the glass.
He had an idea. He had a vision of a view
of Philadelphia that I couldn't see through.
I can see him tapping with a hammer
at the house, making a space for the wind,
then his hand, then enough to perch his thin body
on working and fuming in the red brick dust, enamored
of his husbandry, when he fell headfirst into the line
my mother strung for clothes, righted himself before his destiny,
brushed himself off, became the window, the stain in the glass, the
    irony.

Alberto Ríos

Sleeping on Fists

Humbly resolving to pray that God
should deliver him from evil thoughts
his head struck the ground as the woman
began hauling him along by the legs.
His uncombed head felt like one
in a bunch of fibrous coconuts
that ladies might buy along the road,
and felt also like the sting moment
his chipped Toledo blade physically
struck open one of those milk heads.
Things in fact felt here like
the state of life one imagines to exist
in the sea: wet and slow and nauseous
with the liquid soft slap after slap
undertow of waves in the insolid middle
of the seas at storm, or at wind.
But after speculation came reality.
Directly down at him her head raised
a clam and lofty eye, that exactly.
And she withdrew without lowering
even her shawl, slowly, evenly pacing,
nauseously counting out precious steps
as if measuring thereby her misfortune
along the length of the room.
But his own eyes raised then fell
as if the cords that held them taut
had been severed suddenly, he imagined,
like carrots for the evening meal,
both eyes at the same instant useless,
half-eyes, half-men.
Inside he turned sadly to himself:
This is how I embraced your mother
when against her wishes I went
fiercely to fight in the last war.

And then he sang, to answer himself,
Why do the whores all love me so?
Look at my thumb and look at my toe.

He fell drunk again, and asleep,
like all the other times of celebration,
she thought, that should have been better,
the Christmas, the New Year, the birthday.
He had whispered instead that her eyes
opened like huge and wet, ugly clams
which tried to draw his spirit
into her muscly insides
smooth and soft and disgusting
the way he said her feminine envelope
tried to swallow him up on cold nights.
But he would rather be cold than die.
This was unfair, these comments to her.
She was after all his wife, and he had
chosen her, and this was the truth.
He had measured a hard life
but so had she, harder even—she had
lived with him, had been forced
in some way inside to care.
So this was their way, she nodded.
He to be drunk, and herself
to take charge of him, to pull him
physically out of loose women
and drag him home as if he were a drunk
or a bad man after all, added to
the days he had to live with himself
and with her, her clam and salt eyes.
But these were their functions, she
decided, and all else was without meaning,
the celebration of sadness
must take this form.

Michael Blumenthal

Waving Good-Bye to My Father

My father, folding toward the earth again, plays
his harmonica and waves his white handkerchief
as I drive off over the hills to reclaim my life.

Each time, I am sure it's the last,
but it's been this way now for twenty-five years:
my father waving and playing "Auf Wiedersehen,"
growing thin and blue as a late-summer iris,
while I, who have the heart for love but not
the voice for it, disappear into the day, wiping
the salt from my cheeks and thinking of women.
There is no frenzy like the frenzy of his happiness,
and frenzy, I know now, is never happiness:
only the loud, belated cacophony of a lost soul
having its last dance before it sleeps forever.

The truth, which always hurts, hurts now—
I have always wanted another father: one
who would sit quietly beneath the moonlight,
and in the clean, quiet emanations of some
essential manhood, speak to me of what,
a kind man myself, I wanted to hear.

But this is not a poem about self-pity:

As I drive off, a deep masculine quiet rises,
of its own accord, from beneath my shoes.
I turn to watch my father's white handkerchief
flutter, like an old Hasid's prayer shawl,
among the dark clouds and the trees. I disappear
into the clean, quiet resonance of my own life.

To live, dear father, *is to forgive.*
And I forgive.

Selected Bibliography

James Agee (b. 1909, Knoxville, TN; d. 1955, New York City) *The Collected Poems of James Agee* (Yale University Press, 1968)

A.R. Ammons (b. 1926, Whiteville, NC) *Collected Poems 1951–1971* (W.W. Norton, 1972); *Sphere: The Form of a Motion* (W.W. Norton, 1974); *Diversifications* (W.W. Norton, 1975); *The Snow Poems* (W.W. Norton, 1977); *The Coast of Trees* (W.W. Norton, 1981); *Worldly Hopes: Poems* (W.W. Norton, 1982); *Lake Effect Country* (W.W. Norton, 1983)

John Ashbery (b. 1927, Rochester, NY) *Some Trees* (Yale University Press, 1956); *The Tennis Court Oath* (Wesleyan University Press, 1962); *Rivers and Mountains* (Holt, Rinehart & Winston, 1966); *The Double Dream of Spring* (E.P. Dutton, 1970); *Three Poems* (Viking, 1972); *Self Portrait in a Convex Mirror* (Viking, 1976); *Houseboat Days* (Viking, 1977); *As We Know* (Viking, 1979); *Shadow Train* (Viking, 1982); *A Wave* (Viking, 1984)

Amiri Baraka (b. 1934, Newark, NJ) *Preface to a Twenty Volume Suicide Note* (Totem, 1961); *The Dead Lecturer* (Grove Press, 1964); *Black Magic: Selected Poetry 1961–1967* (Bobbs Merrill, 1969); *In Our Terribleness* (Bobbs Merrill, 1970); *Spirit Reach* (Jihad, 1972); *Hard Facts* (Peoples War, 1976); *Selected Poetry* (William Morrow, 1979)

Ben Belitt (b. 1911, New York City) *The Five-Fold Mesh* (Knopf, 1938); *Wilderness Stair* (Grove Press, 1955); *The Enemy Joy: New and Selected Poems* (University of Chicago Press, 1964); *Nowhere But Light: Poems 1964–1969* (University of Chicago Press, 1970); *The Double Witness: Poems 1970–1976* (Princeton University Press, 1978)

Marvin Bell (b. 1937, New York City) *Things We Dreamt We Died For* (Stone Wall Press, 1966); *A Probable Volume of Dreams* (Atheneum, 1969); *The Escape into You: A Sequence* (Atheneum, 1971); *Residue of Song* (Atheneum, 1974); *Stars Which See, Stars Which Do Not See* (Atheneum, 1977); *These Green-Going-Into-Yellow* (Atheneum, 1982).

Stephen Berg (b. 1934, Philadelphia, PA) *Bearing Weapons* (Cummington Press, 1963); *The Queen's Triangle: A Romance* (Cummington Press, 1970); *The Daughters* (Bobbs Merrill, 1971); *Grief:*

Poems and Versions of Poems (Grossman, 1975); *With Akhmatova at the Black Gates* (University of Illinois Press, 1981)

John Berryman (b. 1914, McAlester, OK; d. 1972, Minneapolis, MN) *Homage to Mistress Bradstreet* (Farrar, Straus & Giroux, 1956); *The Dream Songs* collected in *77 Dream Songs* (Farrar, Straus and Giroux, 1964) and *His Toy, His Dream, His Rest* (Farrar, Straus and Giroux, 1968); *Delusions, Etc.* (Farrar, Straus & Giroux, 1972); *Henry's Fate and Other Poems* (Farrar, Straus & Giroux, 1977)

Frank Bidart (b. 1939, Bakersfield, CA) *Golden State* (Braziller, 1973); *The Sacrifice* (Random House, 1983)

Michael Blumenthal (b. 1949, Vineland, NJ) *Sympathetic Magic* (Watermark Press, 1980); *Days We Would Rather Know* (Random House, 1984)

Robert Bly (b. 1926, Madison, MN) *Silence in the Snowy Fields* (Wesleyan University Press, 1962); *The Light around the Body* (Harper & Row, 1968); *The Teeth Mother Naked at Last* (City Lights, 1970); *Sleepers Joining Hands* (Harper & Row, 1973); *The Morning Glory* (Harper & Row, 1975); *This Body Is Made of Camphor And Gopher Wood* (Harper & Row, 1977); *This Tree Will Be Here for a Thousand Years* (Harper & Row, 1979); *The Man in the Black Coat Turns* (The Dial Press, 1982)

John Malcolm Brinnin (b. 1916, Halifax, Nova Scotia) *The Sorrows of Cold Stones: Poems 1940–1950* (Dodd Mead, 1951); *The Selected Poems of John Malcolm Brinnin* (Little Brown, 1963); *Skin-Diving in the Virgins and Other Poems* (Delacorte Press, 1970)

Paul Carroll (b. 1927, Chicago, IL) *The Luke Poems* (Folette, 1971); *New and Selected Poems* (Yellow Press, 1979)

Hayden Carruth (b. 1921, Waterbury, CT) *The Crow and The Heart, 1946–1959* (Macmillan, 1959); *Nothing for Tigers: Poems 1959–1964* (Macmillan, 1965); *From Snow and Rock, from Chaos: Poems 1965–1972* (New Directions, 1973); *The Bloomingdale Papers* (University of Georgia Press, 1974); *Brothers, I Loved You All* (The Sheep Meadow Press, 1978); *The Sleeping Beauty* (Harper & Row, 1983)

John Ciardi (b. 1916, Boston, MA) *For Instance* (W.W. Norton, 1979); *Selected Poems* (University of Arkansas Press, 1984)

Robert Creeley (b. 1926, Arlington, MA) *Collected Poems* (University of California Press, 1983)

E.E. Cummings (b. 1884, Cambridge, MA; d. 1962, New York City) *Complete Poems, 1913–1962* (Harcourt Brace Jovanovich, 1963); *Etcetera: The Unpublished Poems of E.E. Cummings* (Liveright Publishing Company, 1983)

James Dickey (b. 1923, Atlanta, Ga.) *Poems 1957–1967* (Wesleyan University Press, 1967); *The Eye-Beaters, Blood, Victory, Madness, Buckhead and Mercy* (Doubleday, 1970); *The Zodiac* (Doubleday, 1976); *The Strength of Fields* (Doubleday, 1979); *Puella* (Doubleday, 1982)

Alan Dugan (b. 1923, Brooklyn, NY) *New and Collected Poems: 1961–1983* (Ecco Press, 1983)

Robert Duncan, (b. 1919, Oakland, CA) *Selected Poems* (City Lights, 1959); *Roots and Branches* (Scribners, 1964); *Bending The Bow* (New Directions, 1968); *Tribunals: Passages 31–35* (Black Sparrow Press, 1970); *The Venice Poem* (Prism, 1975); *Ground Work* (New Directions, 1984)

Richard Eberhart (b. 1904, Austin, MN) *Collected Poems 1930–1976* (Oxford University Press, 1976); *Fields of Grace* (Oxford University Press, 1972); *Ways of Light* (Oxford University Press, 1980)

Edward Field (b. 1924, Brooklyn, NY) *Stand Up, Friend, With Me* (Grove Press, 1963); *Variety Photoplays* (Grove Press, 1967); *A Full Heart* (The Sheep Meadow Press, 1977); *Stars in My Eyes* (The Sheep Meadow Press, 1977)

Allen Ginsberg (b. 1926, Newark, NJ) *Howl and Other Poems* (City Lights, 1956); *Kaddish and Other Poems 1958–1960* (City Lights, 1961); *Reality Sandwiches* (City Lights, 1963); *Planet News 1961–1967* (City Lights, 1968); *The Fall of America* (City Lights, 1972); *Mind Breaths* (City Lights, 1978); *Plutonium Ode* (City Lights, 1982).

Paul Goodman (b. 1911; New York City; d. 1972, New York City) *Collected Poems* (Random House, 1977)

Donald Hall (b. 1928, New Haven, CT) *Exiles and Marriages* (Viking, 1955); *The Dark Houses* (Viking, 1958); *A Roof of Tiger Lilies* (Viking, 1964); *The Alligator Bride: New and Selected Poems* (Harper & Row, 1969); *The Yellow Room Love Poems* (Harper & Row, 1971); *The Town of Hill* (Godine, 1975); *Kicking the Leaves* (Harper & Row, 1978)

Daniel Halpern (b. 1945, Syracuse, NY) *Traveling On Credit* (Viking, 1972); *Street Fire* (Viking, 1975); *Life Among Others* (Viking, 1978); *Seasonal Rights* (Viking, 1982)

Michael S. Harper (b. 1938, Brooklyn, NY) *Dear John, Dear Coltrane* (University of Pittsburgh Press, 1970); *History Is Your Own Heartbeat* (University of Illinois Press, 1971); *Song: I Want a Witness* (University of Pittsburgh Press, 1972); *Debridement* (Doubleday, 1973); *Nightmare Begins Responsibility* (University of Illinois Press, 1974); *Images of Kin: New and Selected Poems* (University of Illinois Press, 1977); *Healing Song for the Inner Ear* (University of Illinois Press, 1983)

Jim Harrison (b. 1937, Greyling, MI) *Plain Song* (W.W. Norton, 1965); *Locations* (W.W. Norton, 1968); *Outlayer & Ghazals* (Simon & Schuster, 1971); *Selected and New Poems 1961–1981* (Delacorte Press, 1982)

Robert Hayden (b. 1913, Detroit, MI; d. 1980, MI) *The Angel of Ascent: New and Selected Poems* (Liveright, Publishing Company, 1975); *American Journal* (Effendi Press, 1978)

Anthony Hecht (b. 1923, New York City) *A Summoning of Stones* (Macmillan, 1954); *The Hard Hours* (Atheneum, 1967); *Millions of Strange Shadows* (Atheneum, 1977); *The Venetian Vespers* (Atheneum, 1979)

John Hollander (b. 1929, New York City) *A Crackling of Thorns* (Yale University Press, 1958); *Movie-Going and Other Poems* (Atheneum, 1962); *Visions From the Ramble* (Atheneum, 1965); *Types of Shape* (Atheneum, 1969); *The Night Mirror* (Atheneum, 1971); *Tales Told of The Fathers* (Atheneum, 1975); *Reflections on Espionage* (Atheneum, 1976); *Spectral Emanations: New and Selected Poems* (Atheneum, 1978) *Blue Wind and Other Poems*

(Johns Hopkins University Press, 1979); *Powers of Thirteen* (Atheneum, 1982)

Richard Hugo (b. 1932, Seattle, WA; d. 1982, MT) *Making Certain It Goes On: The Collected Poems of Richard Hugo* (W.W. Norton, 1984)

David Ignatow (b. 1914, Brooklyn, NY) *Poems 1934–1969* (Wesleyan University Press, 1970); *Facing the Tree* (Little Brown, 1975); *Selected Poems* (Wesleyan University Press, 1975); *Tread the Dark* (Little Brown, 1978); *Whisper to the Earth* (Little Brown, 1982)

Randall Jarrell (b. 1914, Nashville, TN; d. 1965, Greensboro, NC) *Complete Poems* (Farrar, Straus & Giroux, 1969)

Robinson Jeffers (b. 1887, Pittsburgh, PA; d. 1962, CA) *Selected Poems* (Knopf, 1965)

Donald Justice (b. 1925, Miami, FL) *The Summer Anniversaries* (Wesleyan University Press, 1960); *Night Light* (Wesleyan University Press, 1967); *Sixteen Poems* (Stone Wall Press, 1970); *Departures* (Atheneum, 1973); *Selected Poems* (Atheneum, 1979)

Milton Kessler (b. 1930, Brooklyn, NY) *A Road Came Once* (Ohio State University Press, 1963); *Sailing Too Far* (Harper & Row, 1973); *Sweet Dreams* (Black Bird Press, 1979)

Galway Kinnell (b. 1927, Providence, RI) *Body Rags* (Houghton Mifflin, 1968); *The Book of Nightmares* (Houghton, Mifflin, 1971); *The Avenue Bearing the Initial of Christ Into the New World: Poems 1946–1964* (Houghton Mifflin, 1974); *Mortal Acts, Mortal Words* (Houghton, Mifflin, 1981); *Selected Poems* (Houghton Mifflin, 1982)

Etheridge Knight (b. 1931, Corinth, MI) *Poems from Prison* (Broadside Press, 1968); *Belly Song and Other Poems* (Broadside Press, 1973); *Born of a Woman: New and Selected Poems* (Houghton, Mifflin, 1981)

Stanley Kunitz (b. 1905, Worcester, MA) *The Poems of Stanley Kunitz 1928–1978* (Little Brown, 1979); *The Wellfleet Whale and Companion Poems* (The Sheep Meadow Press, 1983)

Philip Levine (b. 1928, Detroit, MI) *On the Edge* (Stone Wall Press, 1963); *Not This Pig* (Wesleyan University Press, 1968); *They Feed That Lion* Atheneum, 1972); *The Names of the Lost* (Atheneum, 1976); *7 Years from Somewhere* (Atheneum, 1979) *Ashes: Poems New and Old* (Atheneum, 1979); *One for the Rose* (Atheneum 1981); *Selected Poems* (Atheneum, 1984)

Larry Levis (b. 1946, Fresno, CA) *Wrecking Crew* (University of Pittsburgh, 1972); *The Afterlife* (University of Iowa, 1977); *The Dollmaker's Ghost* (E.P. Dutton, 1981)

Laurence Lieberman (b. 1935, Detroit, MI) *The Unblinding: Poems* (Macmillan, 1968); *The Osprey Suicides* (Macmillan, 1973); *God's Measurements* (Macmillan, 1980); *Eros at the World Kite Pageant: Poems 1979–1982* (Macmillan, 1983)

John Logan (b. 1923, Red Oak, IA) *Cycle for Mother Cabrini* (Grove Press, 1955); *Ghost of the Heart* (University of Chicago Press, 1960); *Spring of the Thief: Poems 1960–1962* (Knopf, 1963); *The Zig-Zag Walk: Poems 1963–1968* (E.P. Dutton); *The Anonymous Lover* (Liveright Publishing Company, 1973); *The Bridge of Change* (BOA Editions, 1981); *Only the Dreamer Can Change the Dream* (Ecco Press, 1981)

Robert Lowell (b. 1917, Boston, MA; d. 1977, New York City) *Lord Weary's Castle* (Harcourt Brace Jovanovich, 1946); *The Mills of Kavanaughs* (Harcourt Brace Jovanovich, 1951); *Life Studies* (Farrar, Straus & Giroux, 1959); *For the Union Dead* (Farrar, Straus & Giroux, 1964); *Near the Ocean* (Farrar, Straus & Giroux, 1967); *History* (Farrar, Straus & Giroux, 1973); *Selected Poems* (Farrar, Straus and Giroux, 1976); *Day by Day* (Farrar, Straus and Giroux, 1977)

Thomas Lux (b. 1946, MA) *The Glassblower's Breath* (Cleveland State University Press, 1976); *Sunday* (Houghton Mifflin, 1980)

Paul Mariani (b. 1940, New York City) *Timing Devices* (Godine, 1980); *Crossing Cocytus* (Grove Press, 1982)

James Merrill (b. 1926, New York City) *First Poems* (Knopf, 1951); *The Country of a Thousand Years of Peace and Other Poems* (Knopf, 1959); *Water Street* (Atheneum, 1962); *Nights and Days*

(Atheneum, 1966); *The Fire Screen* (Atheneum, 1969); *Braving the Elements* (Atheneum, 1972); *Divine Comedies* (Atheneum, 1976); *Mirabell: Books of Numbers* (Atheneum, 1978); *The Changing Light at Sandover* (Atheneum, 1982); *From the First Nine: Poems 1946–1976* (Atheneum, 1982)

W.S. Merwin (b. 1927, New York City) *The Carrier of Ladders* (Atheneum, 1970); *Writings to an Unfinished Accompaniment* (Atheneum, 1974); *The First Four Books of Poems* (Atheneum, 1975); *The Compass Flower* (Atheneum, 1977); *Opening the Hand* (Atheneum, 1983)

Robert Mezey (b. 1935, Philadelphia, PA) *The Door Standing Open: New and Selected Poems 1954–1969* (Houghton Mifflin, 1970)

Howard Moss (b. 1922, New York City) *The Winter Come, A Summer Gone: Poems 1946–1960* (Scribners, 1960); *Finding Them Lost and Other Poems* (Scribners, 1965); *Second Nature* (Atheneum, 1968); *Selected Poems* (Atheneum, 1971); *Buried City* (Atheneum, 1975); *A Swim Off the Rocks: Light Verse* (Atheneum, 1976); *Tigers and Other Lilies* (Atheneum, 1977); *Notes From the Castle* (Atheneum, 1979); *Rules of Sleep* (Atheneum, 1984)

Stanley Moss (b. 1925, New York City) *The Wrong Angel* (Macmillan, 1966); *Skull of Adam* (Horizon Press, 1979)

Howard Nemerov (b. 1920, New York City) *The Collected Poems of Howard Nemerov* (University of Chicago Press, 1977)

Frank O'Hara (b. 1926, Baltimore, MD; d. 1966, New York City) *Collected Poems* (Knopf, 1971); *Early Poems 1946–1951* (Grey Fox Press, 1976); *Poems Retrieved 1951–1966* (Grey Fox Press, 1977)

George Oppen (b. 1908, New Rochelle, NY) *The Collected Poems of George Oppen 1929–1975* (New Directions, 1975)

Gil Orlovitz (b. 1918, Philadelphia, PA; d. 1955, PA) *Selected Poems* (Inferno Press, 1960); *Art of the Sonnet* (Hilsboro Publications, 1961)

Robert Pack (b. 1929, New York City) *The Irony of Joy* (Scribners, 1955); *A Stranger's Privilege* (Macmillan, 1959); *Guarded by Women* (Random House, 1963); *Home From the Cemetery* (Rutgers University Press, 1969); *Nothing But Light* (Rutgers University Press, 1972); *Keeping Watch* (Rutgers University Press, 1976); *Waking to My Name: New and Selected Poems* (Johns Hopkins University Press, 1980)

Stanley Plumly (b. 1939, Barnesville, OH) *In the Outer Dark* (Louisiana State University Press, 1970); *Giraffe* (Louisiana State University Press, 1973); *Out-of-the-Body Travel* (Ecco Press, 1977); *Summer Celestial* (Ecco Press, 1983)

David Ray (b. 1932, Sapula, OK) *X-Rays* (Cornell University Press, 1965); *Dragging the Main and Other Poems* (Cornell University Press, 1968); *Gathering Firewood: New Poems and Selected* (Wesleyan University Press, 1974); *The Tramp's Cup* (Chariton Press, 1978)

James Reiss (b. 1941, New York City) *The Breathers* (Ecco Press, 1974); *Express* (University of Pittsburgh Press, 1983)

Charles Reznikoff (b. 1894, Brooklyn, NY; d. 1976, New York City) *Poems 1918–1936: The Complete Poems of Charles Reznikoff* (Black Sparrow Press, 1978); *Poems 1937–1975: The Complete Poems of Charles Reznikoff, Vol. 2* (Black Sparrow Press, 1978)

Alberto Ríos (b. 1952, NM) *Whispering to Fool the Wind* (The Sheep Meadow Press, 1981)

Theodore Roethke (b. 1908, Saginaw, MI; d. 1963, WA) *Collected Poems* (Doubleday, 1966)

Michael Ryan (b. 1946, PA) *Threats Instead of Trees* (Yale University Press, 1974); *In Winter* (Holt Rinehart & Winston, 1982)

Ira Sadoff (b. 1945, New York City) *Settling Down* (Houghton Mifflin, 1975); *Palm Reading in Winter* (Houghton Mifflin, 1978)

Philip Schultz (b. 1945, Rochester, NY) *Like Wings* (Viking, 1978); *Deep Within the Ravine* (Viking, 1984)

Delmore Schwartz (b. 1913, Brooklyn, NY; d. 1966, New York City) *Selected Poems: Summer Knowledge* (New Directions, 1959); *The Last and Lost Poems of Delmore Schwartz* (The Vanguard Press, 1979)

Harvey Shapiro (b. 1924, Chicago, IL) *The Eye* (Swallow Press, 1953); *Mountain, Fire, Thornbush* (Swallow Press, 1961); *Battle Report: Selected Poems* (Wesleyan University Press, 1966); *This World* (Wesleyan University Press, 1971); *Lauds* (Sun Press, 1975); *Lauds and Nightsounds* (Sun Press, 1978)

Karl Shapiro (b. 1913, Baltimore, MD) *Collected Poems* (Random House, 1978)

Charles Simic (b. 1938, Yugoslavia) *What the Grass Says* (Kayak, 1967); *Dismantling the Silence* (Braziller, 1971); *Return to a Place Lit by a Glass of Milk* (Braziller, 1974); *Charon's Cosmology* (Braziller, 1977); *Class Ballroom Dances* (Braziller, 1980); *Austerities* (Braziller, 1982)

Louis Simpson (b. 1923, Jamaica, W. I.) *Good News of Death and Other Poems* (Scribners, 1955); *A Dream of Governors* (Wesleyan University Press, 1959); *At the End of the Open Road* (Wesleyan University Press, 1963); *Selected Poems* (Oxford University Press, 1966); *Searching for the Ox* (William Morrow, 1976); *Caviare at the Funeral* (Franklin Watts, 1980); *The Best Hour of The Night* (Ticknor & Fields, 1983)

L.E. Sissman (b. 1928, Detroit, MI; d. 1974, Boston, MA) *Hello, Darkness: The Collected Poems of L.E. Sissman* (Little, Brown, 1978)

Bruce Smith (b. 1949, Philadelphia, PA) *The Common Wages* (The Sheep Meadow Press, 1983)

Dave Smith (b. 1942, Portsmouth, VA) *The Fisherman's Whore* (Ohio State University Press, 1974); *Cumberland Station* (University of Illinois Press, 1976); *Goshawk, Antelope* (University of Illinois Press, 1979); *Dream Flights* (University of Illinois Press, 1981); *In the House of the Judge* (Harper & Row, 1983)

William J. Smith (b. 1918, Winnfield, LA) *Poems 1947–1957* (Little Brown, 1957); *The Tin Can and Other Poems* (Delacorte Press, 1968); *New and Selected Poems* (Delacorte Press, 1970); *Venice in the Fog* (Unicorn Press, 1975); *The Traveler's Tree: New and Selected Poems* (Persea Books, 1981)

W.D. Snodgrass (b. Wilkinsburg, PA) *Heart's Needle* (Knopf, 1960);

After Experience (Harper & Row, 1968); *The Führer Bunker: A Cycle of Poems in Progress* (BOA Editions, 1977); *If Birds Built With Your Hair* (Nadja Press, 1979); *Six Minnesinger Poems* (Burning Deck, 1983)

Gary Snyder (b. 1930, San Francisco, CA) *Myths and Texts* (Totem, 1960); *The Back Country* (New Directions, 1968); *Regarding Wave* (New Directions, 1970); *Turtle Island* (New Directions, 1974); *Axe Handles* (North Point Press, 1983)

David St. John (b. 1949, San Joaquin Valley, CA) *Hush* (Houghton Mifflin, 1978); *The Shore* (Houghton Mifflin, 1980)

William Stafford (b. 1914, Hutchinson, KS) *Stories That Could Be True: New and Collected Poems* (Harper & Row, 1977); *A Glass Face in the Rain* (Harper & Row, 1982); *Smoke's Ways: Poems From Limited Editions* (Greywolf Press, 1983)

Gerald Stern (b. 1925, Pittsburgh, PA) *The Naming of Beasts and Other Poems* (Cummington Press, 1973); *Rejoicings* (Fiddlehead, 1973); *Lucky Life* (Houghton Mifflin, 1977); *The Red Coal* (Houghton Mifflin, 1981)

Wallace Stevens (b. 1879, Reading, PA; d. 1955, Hartford, CT) *Collected Poems* (Knopf, 1954); *Opus Posthumous* (Knopf, 1957)

Mark Strand (b. 1934, Summerside, Prince Edward Island, Canada) *Sleeping with One Eye Open* (Stone Wall Press, 1964); *Reasons for Moving* (Atheneum, 1968); *Darker* (Atheneum, 1970); *The Story of Our Lives* (Atheneum, 1973); *The Sergeantville Notebook* (Burning Deck, 1973); *The Late Hour* (Atheneum, 1978); *Selected Poems* (Atheneum, 1982)

James Tate (b. 1943, Kansas City, MO) *The Lost Pilot* (Yale University Press, 1967); *The Oblivion Ha-Ha* (Little Brown, 1970); *Absences* (Little Brown, 1972); *Viper Jazz* (Wesleyan University Press, 1976); *Riven Doggeries* (Ecco Press, 1979); *Constant Defender* (Ecco Press, 1983)

Robert Penn Warren (b. 1905, Guthrie, KY) *Selected Poems 1923–1943* (Harcourt Brace Jovanovich, 1944); *Promises: Poems 1954–1956* (Random House, 1957); *Selected Poems 1923–1975* (Random House, 1976); *Now and Then: Poems 1976–1978* (Random House, 1978); *Being Here: Poetry 1977–1980* (Random House, 1980); *Have You Ever Eaten Stars: Poems 1979–1980* (Random House, 1981); *Chief Joseph of the Nez Perce* (Random House, 1983)

Theodore Weiss (b. 1916, Reading, PA) *The World Before Us: Poems 1950–1970* (Macmillan, 1970); *Views and Spectacles: New Poems and Selected Shorter Poems* (Macmillan, 1979); *Recoveries* (Macmillan, 1982)

Irving Wexler (b. 1918, New York City) Works published in *Poetry.*

Philip Whalen (b. 1923, Portland, OR) *On Bear's Head: Selected Poems* (Harcourt Brace Jovanovich, 1969); *The Kindness of Strangers: Poems 1969–1974* (Four Seasons, 1975); *Decompressions: Selected Poems* (Grey Fox Press, 1977); *Enough Said: Poems 1974–1979* (Grey Fox Press, 1980)

John Hall Wheelock (b. 1886, East Hampton, NY; d. 1978, New York City) *The Blessed Earth: New and Selected Poems, 1927–1977* (Scribner's, 1977)

John Wheelwright (b. 1897, Boston, MA; d. 1940, Boston, MA) *Collected Poems* (New Directions, 1983)

Richard Wilbur (b. 1921, New York City) *Ceremony and Other Poems* (Harcourt Brace Jovanovich, 1950); *Things of This World* (Harcourt Brace Jovanovich, 1956); *Advice to a Prophet and Other Poems* (Harcourt Brace Jovanovich, 1962); *Walking to Sleep: New Poems and Translations* (Harcourt Brace Jovanovich, 1969); *The Mind-Reader: New Poems* (Harcourt Brace Jovanovich, 1969); *Opposites: Poems and Drawings* (Harcourt Brace Jovanovich, 1979)

C.K. Williams (b. 1936, Newark, NJ) *Lies* (Houghton Mifflin, 1969); *I Am The Bitter Name* (Houghton Mifflin, 1972); *With Ignorance* (Houghton Mifflin, 1977); *Tar* (Random House, 1983)

William Carlos Williams (b. 1883, Rutherford, NJ; d. 1963, Rutherford, NJ) *Collected Earlier Poems* (New Directions, 1951); *Collected Later Poems* (New Directions, 1963)

Robert Winner (b. 1930, New York City) *Green in the Body* (Slow Loris Press, 1979); *Flogging the Czar* (The Sheep Meadow Press, 1983)

Charles Wright (b. 1935, Pickwick Dam, TN) *The Grave of The Right Hand* (Wesleyan University Press, 1970); *Hard Freight* (Wesleyan University Press, 1973); *Bloodlines* (Wesleyan University Press, 1975); *China Trace* (Wesleyan University Press, 1977); *Country Music* (Random House, 1982)

James Wright (b. 1927, Martin's Ferry, OH; d. 1980, New York City) *Collected Poems* (Wesleyan University Press, 1971); *Two Citizens* (Farrar, Straus & Giroux, 1974); *To a Blossoming Pear Tree* (Farrar, Straus & Giroux, 1977); *This Journey* (Random House, 1982)

Jay Wright (b. 1936, New York City) *Dimensions of History* (Kayak, 1976); *Homecoming Singer* (Corinth Books, 1979); *The Double Invention of Komo* (University of Texas Press, 1980)

Paul Zweig (b. 1941, Brooklyn, NY) *Against Emptiness* (Harper & Row, 1971); *Dark Side of the Earth* (Harper & Row, 1974)

Note on the Editor

Jason Shinder was born in 1955, in Brooklyn. He is the author of the poetry collection, *End of the Highest Balcony* (Indiana-Purdue University). He presently directs The Writer's Voice of the West Side YMCA in New York City, is interim director of The Poetry Society of America, and is a lecturer for The Learning to Read through the Arts Program at the Guggenheim Museum.

Acknowledgments

Agee, James: "In Memory of My Father," from *The Collected Poems of James Agee.* Copyright © 1962, 1968 by the James Agee Trust. Reprinted by permission of Houghton Mifflin Company.

Ammons, A.R.: "My Father Used to Tell of an" is reprinted from *The Snow Poems* by A.R. Ammons, by permission of the author and the publisher, W.W. Norton & Company, Inc. Copyright © 1977 by A.R. Ammons.

Ashbery, John: "A Boy" is reprinted from *Some Trees* by John Ashbery. Reprinted by permission of Yale University Press. Copyright © 1956.

Baraka, Inamu Amiri: "The Ballgame" is reprinted by permission of the author.

Belitt, Ben: "Karamazov" is reprinted by permission of the author. This poem first appeared in *Salmagundi.* Reprinted from *Wilderness Stair.* Copyright © 1955 by Grove Press.

Bell, Marvin: "Letting in Cold" in *Things We Dreamt We Died For.* Copyright © The Stone Wall Press. Reprinted by permission of the author and Stone Wall Press. "Treetops" in *A Probable Volume of Dreams.* Copyright © 1969. Reprinted with the permission of Atheneum Publishers. "To an Adolescent Weeping Willow" in *These Green-Going-to-Yellow.* Copyright © 1981. Reprinted with the permission of Atheneum Publishers.

Berg, Stephen: "For My Father" is reprinted from *Grief* by Stephen Berg. Reprinted by permission of Grossman Publishers. Copyright © 1975.

Berryman, John: "Dream Song (#241)," "Dream Song (#384)" from *Dream Songs.* Copyright © 1959, 1962, 1964, 1965, 1966, 1967, 1968, 1969 by John Berryman. Reprinted with the permission of Farrar, Straus & Giroux.

Bidart, Frank: "Golden State" is reprinted from *Golden State* by Frank Bidart. Copyright © 1973 by Frank Bidart. Reprinted with the permission of George Braziller Publishers.

Bly, Robert: "Finding the Father" from *This Body Is Made from Camphorwood* by Robert Bly. Copyright © 1977 by Robert Bly. Reprinted by permission of Harper & Row Publishers, Inc. "My Father's Wedding" and "For My Son, Noah, Ten Years Old"

291

St. John, David: "Hush" from *Hush* by David St. John. Copyright © 1975, 1976 by David St. John. Reprinted by permission of Houghton Mifflin Company.

Stafford, William: "My Father: October, 1942" is reprinted from *Stories That Could Be True* by William Stafford. Copyright © 1977 by William Stafford. Reprinted with the permission of Harper & Row Publishers.

Stern, Gerald: "The Sensitive Knife" from *Lucky Life* by Gerald Stern. Copyright © 1977 by Gerald Stern. Reprinted by permission of Houghton Mifflin Company. "The Dancing" is reprinted with the permission of the author.

Stevens, Wallace: "The Irish Cliffs of Moher" is reprinted from *Collected Poems* by Wallace Stevens. Copyright © 1954 by Wallace Stevens. Reprinted with the permission of Random House, Inc.

Strand, Mark: "Elegy for My Father" in *The Story of Our Lives*. Copyright © 1978 by Mark Strand. Reprinted with the permission of Atheneum Publishers.

Tate, James: "The Pilot" is reprinted from *The Lost Pilot* by James Tate. Copyright © 1967 by James Tate and Yale University Press. Reprinted with the permission of the author.

Warren, Robert Penn: "After Night Flight" and "Promises" reprinted from *Selected Poems 1923–1975*. Copyright © 1976 by Robert Penn Warren. Reprinted with the permission of Random House, Inc.

Weiss, Theodore: "The Death of Fathers" is reprinted with the permission of the author. This poem first appeared in *Tri-Quarterly*, Vol. 55 (Fall 1982).

Wexler, Irving: "Elegy for My Father (Part VIII)" is reprinted with the permission of the author.

Whalen, Philip: "For My Father" is reprinted from *On Bear's Head*. Reprinted with the permission of the author.

Wheelock, John Hall: "The Gardener" (copyright © 1957 John Hall Wheelock) in *By Daylight and in Dreams* Copyright © 1970 John Hall Wheelock. Reprinted with the permission of Charles Scribner's Sons. "The Gardener" was first published in *The New Yorker*.

292

Other titles from The Sheep Meadow Press:

Peter Balakian
> *Father Fisheye*
> *Sad Days of Light*

Chana Bloch
> *Secrets of the Tribe*

Hayden Carruth
> *Brothers, I Loved You All*

Arthur Gregor
> *Embodiment and Other Poems*

David Ignatow
> *Leaving the Door Open*
> *The Notebooks of David Ignatow*

David Jones
> *The Roman Quarry*

Stanley Kunitz
> *The Wellfleet Whale and Companion Poems*

Jacov Lind
> *The Stove*

F.T. Prince
> *Collected Poems*
> *Later On*
> *The Yüan Chên Variations*

Dahlia Ravikovitch
> *A Dress of Fire*

Alberto Ríos
> *Whispering to Fool the Wind*